BLUEGRASS WASTELAND

BLUEGRASS WASTELAND

T.R.Hummer

SELECTED POEMS

Arc
PUBLICATIONS
2005

Published by Arc Publications
Nanholme Mill, Shaw Wood Road
Todmorden, Lancs OL14 6DA, UK

Design by Tony Ward

Printed and bound by Antony Rowe Ltd, Eastbourne

ISBN-13: 978 1 900072 82 0
ISBN-10: 1 900072 82 3

Poems in this collection have
previously been published in

The Angelic Orders (Louisiana State University Press, 1982)
The Passion of the Right-Angled Man (University of Illinois Press, 1984)
Lower Class Heresy (University of Illinois Press, 1987)
The 18,000-Ton Olympic Dream (Morrow, 1991)
Walt Whitman in Hell (Louisiana State University Press, 1996)
Useless Virtues (Louisiana State University Press, 2001)

The poems 'Blood Oranges', 'Ring Cycle', 'Soft Money',
'Telepathic Poetics', 'The End of History' and 'Axis' are reprinted
by permission of Louisiana State University Press from *Useless
Virtues: Poems* by T. R. Hummer
(copyright © 2001 by T. R. Hummer)

Cover painting:
'Bluegrass Wasteland' by Ivan Appelrouth
© Ivan Appelrouth 2005

The publishers acknowledge financial
assistance from Arts Council England, Yorkshire

Arc Publications International Poets
Series Editor: John Kinsella

Every work turns against its author: the poem will crush the poet, the system the philosopher, the event the man of action... One always perishes by the self one assumes: to bear a name is to claim an exact mode of collapse.
    – E. M. Cioran

For Theo and Jackson

Contents

Selected Lyric and
Shorter Narrative Poems
2001-1982

from USELESS VIRTUES (2001)

Domestic Lyric

He washes the dishes. He does the laundry,
   bleaching by hand something delicate
And white in the bathroom sink. He sits

   at the kitchen table reading. Nothing of her
In the house but a resonant emptiness. A garbage truck
   shifts gears in the vacant morning street,

While a hundred miles to the east, the Atlantic
   eats into its own shoreline
Until whole streets of overpriced ocean-front

   split-levels begin to collapse. *I'll call,*
She said on her way out the door. That
   was years ago. As decades develop, he feels

The quality of his ignorance grow richer. Wars
   come closer. He hears cannons in the mountains,
The scream of a horse with shrapnel in its throat,

   the guttural thump of an Anglo-Saxon axe
Splitting a shoulder bone. He stirs a pot of soup,
   adds lentils and pepper to taste. He shuffles

A stack of mail: her boxholders, a magazine.
   At the moment his death arrives,
He is polishing silver: A stylized effigy of the sun.

   She wears it sometimes as a pin,
Or makes a pendant of it – either way he can see
   his own face distorted in its brilliant thorax.

There is fire, a famine, continental drift.
   The garbage truck grinds again.
Even dead, he remembers to lower the toilet seat

   and check all the locks. *You look younger*, whispers the priest.
I am, he wants to answer, tracing the small prints
   of a woman's hand in dust on the sarcophagus.

Blood Oranges

They are eating blood oranges
    on the broken fire escape.
Blood oranges – what makes us want
    to say that? A boy and his mother,

Quietly eating blood oranges.
    Behind them, in the apartment,
Another china plate smacks against the wall.
    The last plate, the mother knows.

She's been counting. Next will come
    the soup tureen, gravy boat,
Heavy serving dishes. The boy drops
    bits of peel into the alley underneath them.

Two stories down, they detonate in afternoon light
    while ice on the pitted iron grid
Of the platform implodes inversely.
    At least she has saved the one bowl,

This one, where blood orange segments lie.
    Who knew her grandmother would leave
Her this? Who knew how the war would end?
    Inside, the husband comes to salt

And pepper shakers, not so easily broken.
    He throws them again and again.
Bone china. Blood oranges. In this moment
    the names are sacramental,

A domestic transubstantiation. The boy
    looks out into the contusion
Of the gathering sunset and kicks
    the ladder of the fire escape,

Years since rusted through.
    He learned this from his father,
As he learned in school *Of all the beautiful
    cities on earth, the most beautiful is ours* –

As he learned from God the blood
    of the orange is the blood of God,
The ice of the fire escape is the ice
    of God, the growing darkness

In the alley is the darkness of God, growing.
    It is winter and God is cold.
From the northernmost province of Paradise,
    he can hear the apartment wall

Shattering saucers and cups. He almost
    remembers that anger, or something
Exactly like it. The innocents. A bowl
    of blood. The jawbone of an ass.

Ring Cycle

At the crematorium, the story goes, they gave him
    the ring he had bought for her,
White gold with constellations of tiny diamonds,
    a row of square-cut sapphires
In a black hole at its core. What would he do

    with it now? At home he opened the urn,
Dumped the ashes on the kitchen table, buried
    the ring at the place where he set
Her plate so many mornings – all gone up
    in a greasy smoke now, into

The disinterested abstraction of sky.
    When they cooked together, she loved
Complex flavours, Oaxacan moles with roasted tomatillos,
    deep ragouts of winter roots, cardamom, dark sauce
With garam masala. Often when he thought of her,

it was as a visible aroma of ground
Coriander and allspice. He touched the stove,
    touched the iron pans on their hooks,
The sieve, baker's peel, baking stone. He brought down
    bottles from cabinets, bundles of dried herbs

From the pantry, fresh ones from the crisper drawer.
    He dumped everything on top of the ashes.
With her scarred wooden spoon, patiently, he stirred
    white peppercorns, turmeric, rosemary,
Spanish saffron, blending carefully with carbon,

    teeth, and the irreducible bits of bone –
Then took it up in double handfuls, threw it
    into the ceiling fan, closing his eyes, breathing.
It's like all your stories, she said then, giving him
    her characteristic sidelong smirk:

Sentimental and thin. You're absolutely right,
    he answered, *as usual*, blinking at the nebulous
Sparkle on her finger while he sat
    finally down beside her the way

Soft Money – 10/31/97

An American moon tonight. It renounces its own
    definition. It lights the sidewalk cinematically –
Scatters dramatic chiaroscuro, as if a war is imminent,
    as if this nightclub's facade conceals a resistance cell.

And don't we love the moon in wartime, isn't the brown-out
    seductive, the wound, the disguise? On the corner,
One man is dressed as a freedom fighter. He tells
    an endless joke to his brother the bombardier,

His comrade the amputee. It is late October,
    almost time for the millennium to turn
Angelic. That's a kind of punch line. Children appear
    in sheets, ghosts from a pogrom, laughing.

Then everyone stands aside for the woman in white –
    white gown, white mask of pheasant feathers.
She scatters the crowd and it loves her for her violence.
    Hers is the only real secret here: what she has endured

At the hands of what officers, on what islands,
    in theatres of combat so remote from us
That even the newspaper pales. In the nightclub
    they are playing blues, the 99th empty chorus

Of *Stormy Monday*. A sailor orders a Manhattan,
    and the Nazi bartender stabs a cocktail onion
As the doors swing back. She enters, a windy zeitgeist.
    All intelligence ceases. The teletype clatters into silence.

Here in my chains, in my scars, I might be anyone
    dressed as a quaint Communist or shell-shocked exile.
How is it possible to be this powerfully in love
    with nothing but a moment? I will take my chances

With history, I will lift my hands and beg,
    I will die in a nameless trench with a hole in my throat
You could drive a half-track through. There is moonlight
    translating the silent battlefield into a city

In eastern North America. Across the street, on the wall
    of a bombed-out supermarket, someone has painted
A crude S, like half of a child's swastika. I know
    this woman in the white dress is beyond me.

I see her as if through the window of a troop-train
    where men sleep in an exhausted aura of sweat.
She is standing on the platform of a station in the heart
    of the country, holding her mask in place against the wind.

If she spoke, we might recognize her voice,
    give her a name and forget her, but her camouflage
Is impenetrable. She opens a white beaded bag,
    pulls out a handful of bills. She could own us all.

Telepathic Poetics

To enter them all in darkness, over and over, coming
    through rear windows or baffled front door locks,
Not worried about patrol cars or neighbourhood watch, subverting
    street lights, yard dogs, flowers or any lack of flowers:

To touch whatever is there – jewellery, shells, old letters,
    broken combs, dirty rag dolls, a saxophone on a stand –
Tenderly, as if to steal but not stealing, indiscriminate,
    while the righteous married breathe each others' sleep

In adjoining bedrooms: all this trouble just to be somewhere,
    anywhere, among furniture however polished or broken down,
Among bills, bank statements, death certificates (but none of them
    stamped with our names): in extinguished basements

With fuse boxes, rusted switches invisible, but offering
    at least the possibility of ordinary light.

The End of History – 4/23/94

An ordinary apocalyptic morning
    in the Americas – no earthquakes, no asteroids,
Just the benevolent shadow of a broken promise
    of rain. The adze of Pacific wind
Hones cumulus clouds to nothing. Or does it
    work the other way? And all the newspapers
In the supermarket agree: RICHARD NIXON DEAD.

    The gears of identity turn slow,
But the mesh is implacable. Gone under
    the bonewheel, that spectacular ego, sucked
Down the augers of the absolute. I am choosing
    the best asparagus, I am buying olive oil,
And somewhere that plasticine face, disturbed
    by a permanent stubble, is growing

Even more inhuman. Yes, he was a private citizen,
    yes husband and father, yes nothing more
Than carbon, oxygen, hydrogen. But against
    the overblown blue screen of memory
Napalm flares up on every channel. Bombs
    go off in the vacuum tubes of Saigon.
It is a spring afternoon in liberal Oregon,

    where skinheads shoot stained glass
Out of the façades of synagogues.
    I am writing a check, I am pushing my cart
In a contemplative way through the parking lot.
    I remember that twisted little figure
Beside Mao's ghost in the shadow of the Wall.
    Eisenhower. Kissinger. Hiss. I will not give in

To the fragmentary, I tell myself at the stoplight.
    I will make my language whole. I prepare
A simple pot roast, I scrub the toilet clean.
    Friends come by for dinner, stepchildren
Of clarity, hunted down by the obscure.
    By midnight, I am almost asleep, almost ready
To dream again of our common disaster,

the ratchets of expediency tightening I-beams,
Stroke, stroke, stroke, in the spine, the brain, the heart.
   Time to reinvent humanity, I am thinking,
Time to retool the scrotum and the womb.
   Liar, what do I know, and when
Do I know it? It will be the monotonous
   nightmare again, a thunderhead with the profile

Of a weasel breaking up – or, stalled in the market air
   above us all, one crow blacklisting the wind.

from WALT WHITMAN IN HELL (1996)

Zeitgeist Lightning

What were the doctors doing with old Whitman's brain
When it slipped through their fingers? *Anthropometry,*
The biographers tell us: *the measure of* quote
Man unquote –
           weighing and assessing that most god-
Like tumour of consciousness, mapping out the seat
Of the archangel whose occult name is Genius.
A laboratory worker accidentally
Dropped it on the floor.
              Had he put it in a jar?
He was an intern from Des Moines, say, whose mother
Had pawned, well, anything you care to imagine.
Where was his mind? He sat up late the night before
Rereading *Song of Myself.*
             He knew what he was
Up against. And then the lapse, the hideous mess
On the clinical tile. Will he ever forget
The pure mortification of it? Years pass. Conrad
Writes *Lord Jim*, America elects
               Coolidge, Hoover,
Karloff makes *Frankenstein,* in which the doctor's mad
Assistant drops the normal brain and substitutes
A murderer's – and still that humiliation
Goes through him every time
                he closes his eyes. *Fool,*
The body's own voices accuse: *incompetent.*
He was exhausted, worried, overworked, in debt,
Depressed. All beside the point. His shame defines him.
In the Iowa sky
         lightning leaps its mystic
Synapse. Somewhere a war is starting. Nurses stand
At the bedside holding hypodermics, glucose.
Idiot, destroyer! So this is death at last –
Not at all what he expected –
            more disgusting,
More demeaning. Trucks swarm the highway west of town.
Everything is flattened. Now the doctor tightens
The immaculate bolt in his neck, as the brain –
Whose? – throbs in its bloody rhythm.

                              Yet he can love
Himself completely, even stitched together as
He is. And the rest of us? Where has consciousness
Struck? No matter how we long to drop it, we will
Not crack the convoluted
                              matter of its lines.

Scrutiny

After the D & C, she stood waiting for a taxi
In the clinic awning's shade. It was afternoon in her
Comfortable little city, early rush hour. She could hear
Traffic beginning to swarm under a bloodless bisected moon.
She was watching everything with singular attention,
Men in their wrinkled suits and skin eclipsed by sweat,
The iridescent black of grackles in the gutter, the bright
Chrome and yellow of a 50s Lincoln at the stoplight,
The ambiguous look on the face of God, the shape of her own hands.
And people looked back at her, she thought, with more
Than casual regard, neither sentimental or curious,
But as if they had something disembodied
In common with her. Suddenly she understood how acts
Of attention corrode the world so the flesh feels scraped away,
Worn thin by the action of light, by the eye.
Suddenly she desired another life, a parallel dimension,
Translucent like our own, but in which the dial of consciousness
Is rotated one counterclockwise click, so every mind possesses
The body immediately to the left. At the corner of Second Avenue
And Royal Street, she paid the driver. He watched her as she vanished
Up the steps of the brownstone, a dominion he will never enter,
An allegory whose other side is blankness.

Ohio Abstract: Hart Crane

Factory ether thickens over the milky lake at sunrise,
Imperially, like smoke from the last cigar of the Czar.
Bruised faces of stevedores clarify along the docks
As if a metaphysical fluoroscope were touching them

With infiltrating radiation – on the other side, the skeletal
Shape of a crane appears against white buildings.
The tannery whistle agitates. This is inescapably Cleveland.
It is morning now, and the bridge remains the bridge.

Down by the stockyard fence, a man in a pea coat staggers.
He was up all night drinking dago red. A sailor let him
Suck his dick, then blackmailed him for ten dollars.
Now he'll work sixteen hours in a warehouse shifting

Crates of chocolate hearts stamped out for the glorious balls
Of a second-rate midwestern Gilded Age. It isn't the money
That worries him, the thirty cents an hour. It isn't top hats
Or new puce gloves. He can't forget the synaesthesia,

The luminous foretaste of sweat, those syncopated mystical chimes
In the background of his fumbling at the fly-buttons,
The disciplined, improvised slant rhyme of *denim* and *tongue.*
Blinding, the incense of horseshit in the gutter.

He chokes on the ecstatic rumble of the fourth dimension's junk-carts.
Lonely and stupid and sad, the *Don't you love me?* of the barges.
And what are those great water-birds writing down there the garbage?
In this illusion of space, nothing could ever have existed.

Wrong sex. Wrong sense. Wrong city. Wrong bridge. Wrong life.
But who needs another elegy? No one ever dies here either.
It just goes on and on, gold foil on an assembly line, two tons
Of hearts for New York City. *Metaphor,* riffs the streetcar,

Is *bear over* in the literal Greek. But who says *what*
Or *how heavy?* Blackjack. Crowbar. Hammer. A man
Coldcocked by the shadow of a telephone pole. Think of all they tell you
The soul holds up in the men's room of the Tower of Light.

Maybe nothing ever meant more on earth than what it weighs.

St. Augustine

I was looking for the return of the body's story, a radical sunrise,
Starbursts over the estuary where fishing boats chafed the yachts –
But I only saw the city's brilliant towers, refinery lights wasting
Silver in the predawn essences. None of us had understood.
In the brain, there is a sensitive blister of images we call the lesion of light.
If I close my eyes on a morning in Florida, I can focus the bed
With its abstract tracery of sheets, the fanatical hotel paintings, the lovers
Still *in coitus,* the woman superior, both of them magisterially lonely.
What I remember is memory itself, breath, the tongue on the skin
Of the thigh, a shadow surrounding the furniture, something that is not
Precisely darkness, but an absence more pure, colourless,
The echo of the blind spot. Confession never happens in the dark.
There is always the naked blinding bulb dangled from the black cliché
Of the cord, the fist and its afterglow. I was talking about my life
In the metropolis of assassins, I was tied to the bed with golden ropes,
And the questions never stopped, the tying and untying of knots.
In the parking lot 27 floors below my hotel balcony, in the middle of the night,
A man beat a woman senseless and stole her empty purse.
When morning finally blew in, there were primitive herons mixed up in it,
Astonishing birds the stormy colour of ocean, with wingspans wide
As a nine-year-old is tall: real birds, but the sort of image I could believe
Rises out of the deepest caves of memory when a blackjack cracks the skull.
Who knows what happens after the brain shuts down?
If you're lucky a thumbprint will glow on the plate glass door
In sunlight, the colour of ectoplasm. If you aren't, that song you danced to
In the bar last night will turn up on the elevator's tape loop.

Over the water now, in a sky like the side of a mackerel,
A quarter-moon offers one of its half-lives to the bodiless sunrise,
A celestial residue smeared on the city morning. Seven Stars of David
Painted graffiti yellow on the firmament of asphalt liquefy
In the criminal atmospherics of sidewalks' corruption and acidic dew.
A cruiser circles the pavement, its blue strobe corrosive and clean.
But what did the saints have left when their eyes dissolved in holy light?
Nobody's left to testify. The evidence washes away.
Take everything, somebody whispers. *I'll give you anything.*

First Assembly of God

What was it, crosstown, where the bluesman blew riff after riff
And rattled his cup on the curbing, moaning, that made you
Snatch off your cap and look up there, mouth open, breath in the steel
Air of Chicago childhood rising like a Sunday School image of prayer?
You were the one I loved then, the way I wanted to love

Girls on the tenement steps, bums on the corners:
With a godlike purity I no longer understand, an oceanic feeling,
Everything taken literally. It was you who saw it first. How can I tell you
I have long forgotten your name when your image is with mealways, uplift
Of chin, pulse in the neck, strong line of nose in profile, cap crushed

In one hand against your heart, looking up and pointing?
Three storeys over the street where gangster cars and sepia horses merged,
It glared its bitterness, red paint strafed against brownstone,
FIRST ASSEMBLY OF GOD. You see how it all comes back, like music: 1934.
We walked those freezing Saturdays needing the bodies of men,

Wanting heat, wanting work. That year there was sweat in the factories,
Sweat in the dark of the slaughterhouse and the groins of the fathers.
And there we were, whatever our names, useless and broke the street.
What were we, ten? In some other life, I tell you how much I want you
To lower your hand and turn to me. But you pointed up,

You stared, you said *So that's what Protestants do,*
And told me the vision it gave you, an angelic assembly line
Where hieratic ranks of the proletariat hoisted their shining tools
As enormous organs and limbs made their way down the belt, God's body still
In its elemental forms: primitive elbow joints, ur-vertebrae, eternities

Of nerves and pipelike capillaries wound on miraculous spools the greasy
Rush of furnaces in the tunnels of the small intestine,
The lobes of the liver and the mirror-image lobes of the brain
And the circuitry that connects them, the host of crated hands
With their isinglass nails, the nipples in Cosmoline, bolts, the oily nuts,

The inevitable genitalia broken down and packed in excelsior and silk,
All bearing for the first assembly. *My god, there's work for a man,*
You said, your face with its wind-chapped skin alight with the living blood,
And I thought of the only Jesus I loved, the icon on my Russian uncle's wall,
How the holes in his hands wanted grommeting and the port in his side
wanted seals:

I looked down the street where the first of the marchers lifted
Under the hammer and sickle their *Workers of the World, Unite.*
I wanted to kneel in front of you, I reached for your arm, but you were gone
Into the crowd on the sidewalk where the bluesman's "Love in Vain" was lost
In the noise of boots on concrete, sirens, horses and drums, O brother,

Son of dust, cog in the wheel, archetype lover, man.

My Funny Valentine in Spanish

for Philip Levine

In the 7-11 parking lot, white boys are terrorized
By a Lincoln stereo punching out 98-decibel jazz. The scene
Reminds them unconsciously of high-art cinema shot
In ferocious blue illumination: the deep wax job
Of the Continental telegraphing the lustre of the streetlights,
The stone-coloured lawyer in an elegant linen jacket
Leaning on the fender while the digital self-service pump
Carries on its decisive artifice. Turned up this loud
Past midnight, Miles Davis is a cool apocalypse
Like nothing these boys on stolen skateboards ever entered,
A neighbourhood in which no one remembers the depth
Of the ether where antifreeze and motor oil pool,
Or the white ghosts of congressmen obliterating angels' hairs
With their otherworldly logic. This is the music they play
In the tunnels of the underground where subways run
From Cambodia to East L. A. In the barrios, children speak
The subjunctive – *If this were bread, could one eat it?* –
And the love of God is a drug, like the love of death.
The *abuela* behind the 7-11 counter shuffles
And lays out the cards. Her *abuela* taught her this.
Five of clubs, three of diamonds: every low card
Whispers its password and its alibi. There's an occult
Future here. Somebody makes it. Somebody loves somebody
And crosses the great water for a promise, on a dare.
Rodgers & Hart. The boys on their skateboards listen
To the trumpet whose language nobody taught them.
Mi enamorada graciosa, it might be singing. *Mi corazón.*
One morning somebody wants to blast somebody's lights
Into a pure cobalt vapour floating at the Pleiades' heart,
One morning the cash register and the Lotto machine are eclipsed
By a mist of tear gas-shadowed perfume, the exhaust of the LAPD.
And one morning – Neruda made it past tense in invincible Spanish
That could not translate Franco into hell, or contradict
The bullets that distorted Lorca – *Everything is aflame,*
One morning the fires / Come out of the earth / Devouring people.

The Antichrist in Arkansas

At the edge of town, day lilies the gold of old whiskey
Move tonelessly. At the margin of the courthouse shadow,
A little sky gives off its one unchanging line.
It is written in the Gnostic *Gospel of Truth* that life is nightmare,
As if people were murdering them, though there is no one
Even pursuing them, or they themselves are killing
Their neighbours, for they have been stained with their blood.
Let there be a little clarity here, let the light arrive
The way the dynamite train rolls in from Arkadelphia:
An overwhelming ablution, a scheduled breakdown.
In the crib behind the cotton gin, three of them are gathered.
In the alley off Jefferson Street, they are giving secret signs.
Who are they? Call them the Brotherhood of Darkness.
Give them emblems: khaki workshirts, Prince Albert in a can.
They worship at the Synagogues of the Flesh of the Holy Pig.
Mornings, hours before sunrise, they kneel at the open flame;
Past midnight, if you wake in an impure sweat, you can hear
Their pentatonic psalms sift through the veils of the juke joints.
You who are uninitiate, you who walk the sunlit bricks
Of the Main Street sidewalk past the bank to the hotel café,
You of the regimental necktie, you who render
Unto Woodrow Wilson, live in the obvious houses,
Drive Fords, dance to "Arkansas Traveler" – Brotherhood of Light,
You think the fields at least are innocent, gathered without
The rhetoric of pastoral, the flat farmland, the ploughs
Moving in the middle distance; you believe at least
In the trees, gone in their green brooding. But in 1919,
83 bodies were given to druid oaks on the fringes
Of these blesséd little cities: Conway, Fort Smith, Fayetteville,
West Memphis, El Dorado, Pine Bluff, Forest City,
The mecca of Hot Springs. How many know
The ritual formula that exorcises unclean flesh?
How many have learned the arcana, the knotting
And unknotting of hemp? So it has been written
In *The Paraphrase of Shem*, and quoted
In *The Little Rock Gazette: Nature turned her dark vagina*
And cast from her the power of fire, which was in her
From the beginning, through the practice of darkness.
Look: already the evening brightens, already the locomotive

Crosses the valley in a shimmer of pure entropic heat.
Everything in the flesh converges. In a moment it will be too late.
Gather them up, believer. Put them on the backs of mules.
Take them where the wind completes its broken sentence
Of damnation against the elder, against the ash.
The secret is simplicity: pray to me, the spirit who steals
The breath of the one whose feet no longer touch
The ground; make sacrifice to the god who silences him
Whose testicles bleed in his own unsanctified mouth.

The Heavenly Doctor

Against phthisis. Against hysteria, scoliosis, quinsy.
Acute to the rhythm of the womb's trepidations, morphology of rupture,
Circumcision, leeching, the inhaling of chloroform during labour.
Indentured to disease and infirmity. Dedicated to radical cure.

Against chronic bronchitis and laryngitis: opium smoke.
Against neuralgic affections and rheumatism: the same and again the same.
About death, nobody knows anything, no matter what they tell you.
In Milan, they say a corpse can be consumed in twenty minutes

By a stream of hot air at white heat, for about $3 cost – nothing left
But a little heap of snow-white ashes: As when the meteor passed
In the early morning, and, fading, threw
A sudden glaring into my room like a flash from a hunter's firepan.

Against delirium, the mirrors and smoke of the will.
Case of parturition, ordinary, $50 or more.
Administering an enema, $5. Bleeding, $1. Cupping, $2 or more.
Administration of chloroform during surgical operations, $5 or more.

In this world, saws and the fever – in the next, gauze and morphine.
Against gangrene: amputation. As on the day
The Wadesborough Bridge was cut down and the Spencer Tucker Bridge
Was burnt by order of Colonel Miller, the military commandant,

Whom may the Devil confound for the act.
There on the embankment we found a dozen or more
With inconceivable wounds. I sawed off five arms and six legs
While dragonflies phosphoresced in the breeze on the river

And twelve white herons made the astrologer's wheel in the air overhead.
Against beauty. Against all that beauty portends.
Against any fool who believes in free will or an afterlife.
Against Mysticism, Hedonism, Stoicism, Episcopalianism.

Against heaps of undifferentiated flesh rotting in the sunlight.
In *The London Scalpel,* the world's highest medical authority,
I have read the following, given as an infallible cure
For smallpox and scarlet fever: sulphate zinc, one grain;

Foxglove digitalis, one grain; half a teaspoonful of sugar; mix
With two teaspoonsful of water; take a teaspoonful every hour.
It states that either disease will disappear in half a day.
It states that if countries compelled their doctors to do this,

There would be no need for pesthouses.
Against all such desperate lies, however well-intentioned.
Against nature, corruption of the flesh, the body's subversion.
Against philosophy, which is nothing but the history of our fragmentation.

Against fatherhood, patriots, pride of war, sabre and Minié ball.
Against the human race, which could have ended millennia ago,
Or in any age, by radical celibacy, if everyone on the planet
Would but accede to it. Against knowledge, physical or metaphysical,

Which leads to nothing but this: The soul is flesh. Do as little as you can.
Vis cogitativa, the power of sense: Watch cloud formations change.
Vis rememoritiva, the power of memory: Don't turn your back on your brother.
Brimstone fumes kill every species of fungus in plant, beast, and man.

Case of abortion, actual or threatened only, $25 or more.
Case of syphilis or gonorrhoea, $20 dollars or more *in advance.*
For the blind poor, Rx: bleed. For yourself, Rx: love nothing.
Sow rows of onions only. Plant turnips in the dark of the moon.

Apocatastasis Foretold in the Shape of a Canvas of Smoke

At the left edge of the field of vision, a stooped woman dumps
Steaming water from her galvanized bucket against a granite wall.
In this meditation, she might be an emblem of genocide

Or simply somebody's grandmother dumping dishwater in the snow.
Grey earth, grey sky – the brushstroke of the horizon visible
Only to someone who knows what to look for, pure

Transparent style. The water is a soapy broth of tea dregs,
Grease, and lye, which the wormy dog that hides
Under her skirt licks from the frozen stones. Its every gesture

Is an archetype, something that could be perfectly described only
In Indo-European. In the middle distance, from the indistinct
Shadow of a minor mountain, there is hazy motion, possibly an army:

The sound of leather groaning, silk-muffled hammers
Of the temple builders, adze-chafe, pneumatic saws, the crack
Of a splintering axletree. The dog's ruff is the same shade of silver

As the metal of her bucket, and the water the bucket holds,
And the vapour that rises off the frost-etched stone of the wall.
Her old dress bunches at her belly in an intaglio like stretch marks.

She had children, and those children died. She had children,
And those children had children. Where is the nostalgia
For humanity? Where are all the stories we have learned

To interpret so perfectly? You may think there is tragedy here,
But this is only the beginning. In the gunpowder haze that lifts
Over the boundary-ridge, and in the bucket's mural of steam,

The characters gather: a man who lifts his handful of blood
To the vacuous spirit he knows is his mother, and she drinks
And speaks his name, and is oblivious. Look

Where the machinery of heaven drags form after form
Out of this sarcophagus God carved from the onyx cliff-face of being
And hinged with elaborate craftsmanship into the joinery of her spine,

So when the latch clicks and the lid of her body swings open,
Another rises luminous and whole into the expanse of unconcealment.
It comes almost to nothing. Winter is here, and the half-starved

Cattle still give milk, though it is thin, with a tinge of vein-blue.
February sleet spits on flagstones with the noise a bronze knife makes
Against hickory. The carver at his bench is gouging another bowl

For goats' blood, while the dog in the culvert gnaws
Whatever rat he can find, then curls his carcass in on itself
Like a Möbius strip for warmth, everything drawn together.

from THE 18,000-TON *OLYMPIC DREAM* (1990)

Spring Comes to Mid-Ohio in a Holy Shower of Stars

On the clearest night of the earliest spring of my life,
An Easter Sunday, come in March by the luck of the draw,
I saw a streak of light in the sky like the middle finger of God,
But it did not come down on me. It was the brightness
William James heard about
                  from a housewife-turned-saintly-spiritualist
That she said she always saw when the dead were about to touch her
In that certain way the dead have. I saw it effloresce and vanish.
Standing there on the road next to the blacked-out body of an oak,
I wanted to trance myself into the past, to get in touch
With the ectoplasmic other side.
                I wanted some strangeness to speak
Out of the unpragmatic crystal ball of my larynx and name itself,
In the timbre I whisper to lovers in, my life. But then another
Finger gestured godlike halfway down from the zenith, another, another,
And the sky burned with the print of a whole left hand.
That's the way the past works:
              brilliance, and a slap in the face.
Years later, in winter, when the rusted iron wheels
Of snowploughs gave their spiritual groans in the heat-dead midnight
                      streets,
I would dream God's immaculate body could suddenly be struck
With a human palm the colour of fever, and darken, and die.
But that night in mid-Ohio,
             I knew what the housewife knew
When James sat in her dingy séance parlour with his notebook clumsy
                  on his knee:
That nothing you ever dreamed of saying comes of its own free will.
It has to be beaten out of you, word by impossible word, until the dead
Spread themselves in your flesh like March dogwood spreads through
                      the dark,
And you speak,
      and a stranger writes everything down.

Courtly Love

The candle in the bathroom burns all night
And water in the clawfoot bathtub cools.
It is simple as that. It is clear
This woman and man are lonely and love each other.

Let's say each washed the other clean,
Each lay the other naked
And half asleep on the thick white rug
In the high-ceilinged room of the empty old house

Where I can't help making them lie,
Where in the word *night*
Outside the casement windows
Rain on oak limbs suddenly turn to ice –

As if any of this were more
Than something someone thought of saying,
More than a dream of lost words
We are living through,

The story that goes on being
Mumbled behind the thick
Old-fashioned plaster of the walls
Of a mind we all share, that tries

Again and again to wring out of me
What those older, other lovers
Must have done when they woke stiff
And dew-cold in a forest

With the king her husband's unexpected sword
Between them like the bitter body
Of a child – he rode up while they slept
And laid it there in memory

Of certain honourable truths. But not enough
Remains of the unlikely off-centre ballad
They had to sing to make sense of
Except the white façade

Of this house in mid-Ohio
That fronts a streetful of pickups hissing
Their all-weather tires on the ice,
Conditionally real as the bathroom floor

Where the ancient heraldic lion-footed tub
Spreads its porcelain claws
Beside the blanked-out bodies
Of the two who stir on the white rug now in candlelight,

Dreaming maybe, or – as if the flesh
Of the Western world has a right
To print its darkening
Story on the white page of itself –

In pain a little, a little bruised
Where touch turned to a desperate holding on.

The August Possessions

All over Well, Nevada, numinous desert light
Shivers on the casinos' façades – pink fake adobe,
Neon, snakeskin – and big cars from Dallas and Jersey collapse

Sunstruck over the grease pit of the local Texaco.
At the motel desk they give us a roll of quarters,
Slapped in the palm with the heft of a good blackjack.

Enjoy, they say. And what else is there to do?
Everybody here is a lover, everybody has a secret key
To a bed they've never seen before, everybody has hope,

Even the room service waiter, a skinny man born south of Juarez
Where his youngest sister died foaming a demon from her mouth
Before the priest could come. At noon, when the stalled sun

Raises a coma of heat waves off the parking lot,
He runs from room to room with his heavy tray,
Then hides on break in the everlasting

Twilight of the lounge where drivers of ruptured Lincolns
Wait for shipments of gaskets from Denver.
All of us here know the odds, but the waiter

Takes my elbow, shakes my hand
Off the handle of the slot machine I've fed ten dollars.
He has no papers, his spine has the subtle twist

Of *in utero* malnutrition, but I follow him
To the end of the row, to a machine like all the rest.
This, this, he says, and lays his graceful hands

On the jaundiced lemons of its eyes.
He was twelve years old when his father came in with the priest.
They wiped the epileptic sputum from his sister's face,

Burnt incense and prayed to keep the devils out
Long enough to bury her. No one but Jesus himself
Could promise them more. I balance my chances,

Drop in five quarters, pull the lever, and nothing comes.
The waiter shrugs. *The will of God,* he says.
Why listen to me?

Later, in the dark motel room, the common bed of many strangers
Strains, springs chording under the woman's body
Like tight barbed wire. I touch her face, and I find it

All again, the terror of the random fall
Of money, the leverage of percentages, the unapproachable
Whine of a border patrol airplane, the voice

Of a priest with an ascetically grotesque body
And the hands of an angel commanding me, from the other side
Of the beautiful flesh I have come into, *Begone.*

Slow Train Though Georgia

The mist that rises from this river solidifies the air
Underneath the rusty trestle where a train has come and gone.
It is the precipitate of the chemical morning, dumped
Unceremoniously into the clear solution of a summer night.
Hours earlier, the midnight freight detonated under starlight
Three hours late and thundering toward Birmingham, the red glow
Of the steel mills, the tincture of that constant dawn.
But now the air shuts down. Now the distant whistles of the morning shift
Into the throats of mockingbirds, and the sun works
Its electrolytic clarity from the top down, starting with the ozone.
The mist rising off the muddy little river curves south beyond the bridge.
It follows the water, of which you might be tempted to imagine
It is the astral body, downstream toward the Gulf –
Because you want to believe in the soul of the river, don't you,
You want a name and a positive destination
For this ghostly swath like a scar between banks of new-leafed oaks,
As if the world had a centre and you were standing in it,
As if everything turning were your own self-evident revolution.
But watch this scene long enough and the sun
Will defeat you, the beautiful obscurity of the mist
Will dilute and disappear. Already the revelation is working
Its inevitable way toward you from the upper atmosphere. Soon
The oil-scummed image of the surface of the river will superimpose
Its visionary dreariness on what you can see of the earth:
Red clay, a distant cotton field, the tin roof of a tenant house
Where morning touches a mirror and moves at the constant speed of light
To touch the face of the sleeping man who stirs and touches his wife
Who is awake already, worrying over breakfast, remembering
The deep-night noise of the train that stopped
Whatever dream she might have had, the double blackness
Of coal-heaped gondolas hours after midnight, the anonymous steel
Of wheels against greased rails, inhuman, turning – like everything she knows
About God and politics – against her, going nowhere.

Mississippi 1955 Confessional

It would have been, I think, summer – it would have been August, I think,
Somewhere near midway between solstice and equinox,
When the tractors move all daylight in mirages of their own thrown dust
And the farmhands come in the back gate at noon, empty, with jars in
their hands.
Imagine yourself a child with a fever, half delirious all that month,
And your sisters lift you in your white wooden chair, carry you to the edge
Of a hayfield, set you down in hedgerow shade and leave you
While they go into woods to turn, you think, into swans –
They are so lovely, your sisters, in their white sundresses
That appear and disappear all afternoon among dark trunks of trees.
None of this ever happened. But remember the body heat of the wind
As it came from behind the tenant shack just there on the eastern border
Of your vision to touch you with its loving nigger hand? And there you are,
A white boy brought up believing the wind isn't even human, the wind is
happy
To live in its one wooden room with only newspaper on the walls
To keep out what this metaphor won't now let me call the wind –
But don't worry about that, your sisters in the woods are gathering
Beautiful fruit, you can hear it falling into their hands,
And the big pistons of the tractors drive thunderously home into cylinders
Steel-bright as the future. You are five years old. What do you know?
Your fever is a European delicacy, it burns in your flesh like fate,
A sign from God, cynosure, mortmain, the intricate working out
Of history in the life of the chosen. O listen, white boy, the wind
Has a mythic question only you can answer: *If all men were brothers,*
Would you want your sister to marry one? Let me tell you, white boy, the wind
Is in the woods with its cornmeal and its black iron skillet,
It's playing the blues harp in the poison oak where your youngest sister,
The one with hair so blonde you think it looks like a halo of rain,
Is about to take off her dress. You sit there dreaming your mild fever dream.
You tap your foot to the haybaler's squared rhythms. They've dressed
you in linen.
From the woods where your sisters lie suddenly down, you burn, snow-white.
I've seen your face. I remember your name. I prophesy something you can't
imagine
Is coming to kiss you. And you thought I was reaching back to you in words
To tell you something beautiful, like *wind?*

Austerity in Vermont

Astral blue of old mountains, ridge after rising ridge
Blurring the western horizon just after the sun goes down,
And there, up five degrees, the cold yellow evening star
My almanac says will be Saturn this month, the bastard god nobody
Wants for a father – not much light, but it's all Vermont conceives
Now that September's come and I feel like losing weight.
What is this voice I hear that tells me *Less flesh?*
Where does it go, the meat of the belly, when I stop
Drinking beer and run my groaning mile a day
Into the Yankee wind that articulates a whole
Future of frost in the darkening perpendiculars of maples?
All flesh has a fate, sure enough, though it's clear no body believes
This moment's horoscope, Saturn in the sixth house descending,
Pissed-off cannibal planet of constipation and infanticide –
But what can you do if you're being born right now
In a ward in Burlington? They're about to cut the cord
Just as that point of luminescence the colour of urine on snow
Crowns at the lip of the sky's birth canal. Will you scream
At the doctor to wait just five minutes more with his surgical steel –
Hold on, get back until that terrible light tips over the edge
And dissolves into somebody else's birthday? But look,
It's too late, there's a snip and you're bleeding, your flesh
And your mother's are suddenly lives apart,
And there you lie, naked in that planet's damning radiation.
That's how destiny works – you'll never be a stockbroker.
You'll have five kids of your own, you'll live on a farm in Vermont
Rolling stones up a hill for years until one afternoon you come home
And open fire with your old shotgun on everybody in sight.
Right at the moment, gasping for air, I'm trying to remember
How it felt when the doctor shagged me loose from the rope of blood
That strained me down toward the good sleep of the placenta,
And I was myself apart, zapped from a dozen angles
By all the essences of my future – Mercury, Venus, Mars,
The whole merciless pantheon of necessary acts
That impressed themselves in my blue flesh turning red
With its own bloody weight. And look at me now,
Out on a road in Vermont at sunset, running, trying to choose

To make the bulge in my belly disappear the way my mother did
After the lying-in, after the labour, after the voice
In the anaesthetic stopped its mindless song, and some stranger
Lay there beside her with a body already growing
Ascetic, unbelieving, refusing her, demanding nothing not its own.

Green Mountain Fever

for my daughter

On a ridge above Lake Pleiad, the fresh Caesarian scar
Of a ski slope meanders through the proud flesh of massed autumn maples,
Bringing back the old mother-lie of the earth's bulge –
What was ever born here? – as the mountains metastasize
Their redness in the hydrogen light of another Vermont October afternoon.
Here is a place you can freeze and burn just walking
In and out of shadows, in and out of the wind.
The books say love will be like this, all symptom, untreatable,
But something will come of it, something like what I saw
Years ago in a pulp magazine – *Spontaneous Human Combustion,* caption
                                                              and photo
Of a homey green armchair, cloth etched black with the crude
Unmistakable shape of a human body, clear as on a Nagasaki wall. *True,*
That magazine called itself. I believed. I still want to believe.
I walk softly in this zenith-light, taking my body filled
With phlogiston and napalm gently up the trail to the top of the ridge
Where the ski-lift platform cantilevers over the frost-burnt slope
Down which, after first snow weeks from now, lovers and fools will throw
The bombs of themselves, and something will come of it – snow-blindness,
Adrenaline, unconsciousness, deliverance, broken bones, the quick
Joy of the body, a child born years from now on a January day
In the C-section ward of a southern city where everyone looks up
Suddenly when the snow begins and they have to learn to breathe
Its small quick blades and then heal themselves scarless and sterile.
But I'm wrong. That was all years ago. That was all true.

Now I can stand alone on this platform with its perilous scenic view
And tell myself it's a lie, nobody just explodes, it always takes longer:
Heat and light, yes, but blood too, and the amniotic fluid, and the father-guilt,
And the needle that exorcises peritonitis, and the needle that tries to heal
The uterus and all the intricate layers of muscle and flesh and skin
That, turned inside out, release, yes, a human shape –
And you give it a name that lets you love it like your own –
And that's when the fever starts. So now the body heat
Of the mountains rises and falls, and I stand watching the haze
In the distance clarify as the wind makes its incision,
And when the shadow of a cloud comes over me, I say the names of it all –
Vermont, Green Mountains – as if something could come of the saying,
As if that were a cure, as if just by believing it I could make
The blood in my heart boil to a fine October vapour,
My flesh incandesce in a gestalt of pure oxidation,
And vanish off this mountain absolute and clean, never leaving
Another scar in the shape of myself anywhere in the world again –
That much, you'd think, I could do in the name of love.

from LOWER-CLASS HERESY (1987)

Empty Backstreet in a Small Southern Town

The daughter who has never been here
Will make the connection. It will not be time
For the vine-grip of morning glory –
It will be the rainsilvered winter
You never hear much about, February,

And wind will blow raw down
The left side of a street the rednecks call
Main Street, Niggertown.
She will come here alone, dark-skinned
For a white girl, pitiful

In her unbelief. From the first
House she comes to, the unpainted tin-roofed
Wrack-frame shack, she will hear
Nothing, no hymn-singing mother-voice, no left-
Over cottonfield harmonica, no ghost

Of a pot-bellied white-eyed child
Squealing from a doorway. She would swear
On the whole street, there is nobody home.
This is not what she came here for,
This is not the story

She wanted: no: there will be nothing
To keep her rust-coloured
Hair from blowing loose, nothing to hold
Back the blood-poisoning
Bite of this unexpected

Wind. In her grimace she will look
So much like her mother
It would break your heart if you had one,
If you could know her
Unspoken history of abandonment: but the sun

Will slap its ice-white
Presence on the blacktop,
And nobody will come to explain,
No mammy and no pistol-sagging cop,
Nobody will come to say what

Any of this means, or will ever mean,
In the unfolding human
Heresy of pain.

Cancer Rising

a dream of walking

Maybe this has been done before. Light scatters
Over that ragged western edge of sky he knows
Is trees, hedgerow, wheatfield's boundary, the end of the family
Farm, a border taking on, in this moment's illumination,
The look of a black raw rip
In the tissue of the air,
                              so he knows it is evening,
And he is walking. He has been walking
A long time, maybe hours, or it feels that way.
He does not seem to be going anywhere,
But that does not disturb him. It is winter,
Not a hard freeze, field the dim gold
Of frostbit straw.
                      In this light he could be hanging
From nothing, high in the mild luminosity of the sunset
Itself. He is wearing khaki, its tan the same
Shade as the field's, and he thinks he must be
Invisible here to anything watching,
Even the hard silhouettes of hawks
Turning and falling in the distance,
                                    disappearing, rising,

Appearing, heeling over the edge, out from under the edge,
Of that darkness under the sky. There is nothing
Strange about it. He knows this field. It is the land
He has lived on since he was a boy
Riding bareback on a rope-led mule, hanging
Terrified and mute
                    to the hacked mane while the man
With the halter rope in his hand laughed and would not stop.
He knows he was lifted up to straddle
The mule's high hard spine, knows he suffered like Jesus
In what he barely knew enough to call his balls
At every deliberate mule-step, jolted
Hard over that field of earth turned
                              by the plough for the planter.
But that was then. Now he is walking alone,
The mule dead and the man who led it dead

As Jesus, years. Now nothing lifts him up.
He walks on his own legs, painless, quick
As he ever remembers, no younger than he know
He is, but strong, and he thinks
                    of his wife,
How good it is, when it happens, to find himself suddenly
Able, even at their age, and to find it
As good as it was when they were twenty,
Just married, still childless and amazed:
Good as it was, it is still just as good to touch her,
Still just as good to rise
                    and enter
Invisibility, clear gold of field-light
With a clear sense of time, old enough now to know
What pain means, and what it means to have it
Gone. He turns and looks east, back toward the house with its high-
Ceilinged rooms and polish-blacked
Furniture they say is antique
                    but he knows is only old:
Knows his body lying there in its drugged sleep
Will tremble awake soon enough. She will
Touch his hand, and he will tell her

I had a beautiful dream. I dreamed I was walking.
When he sees her tears, he will regret that he has spoken.
She misunderstands.
                              She thinks it is a sadness
That the mind, dying, dreams what it leaves behind.
But he knows, as he stands looking back at the house lights
And the stars rising above them in the horizon's indigo quick,
That the worlds of dreams are always self created,
And if in his dying the world creates itself again
And gives him back his legs,
                                    strong as they ever lifted him,
That is not grief. The body in that bed she sits beside
Waiting for him to wake regrets everything. But in his dream
He regrets only that he does not know the world so well
He could be sure every detail of it is true:
Grieves he does not know enough about the constellations
To say certainly that the one he sees
                                          scrabbling its slow way
Over the roofbeam, the one he knows enough to call
By its true crab-name, is really where it ought to be:
Because if it is, its obvious symbolism is heavy-handed,
And if it isn't, the dream is all a goddamned lie.
But he finds he cannot remember. If he ever knew,
His memory withholds the answer.
                                    And that is the one true pain,
That there is so much he does not know, like any man:
And that out of the arrogance of men like me, who pretend to know
Anything at all only because they are so afraid of losing
Pain, because they want to go on and on
Touching bodies and dying slow, but never dying,
Ambiguities come to be
                              rearrangements, ironies, mysteries, heresies
Of a man dream-walking a field, or a constellation
With a name that spreads in the breath-clear air
By starry clawpoints, moving dumb, hanging on,
Clinging and ripping at the bellowed lungs of the sky,
Slow-brained in its terror of being, or being lifted there and named
Anything at all by anyone,
                              living or dying.

The Second Story

On the other side of that arc-light-level window
Hung at the top of a slope of Victorian porch,
Someone believes in the laying on of hands,

Or some two believe, and the woman of them sings
Her hymn. It comes down to me where I stand unashamed
To listen, unashamed to be here under these morning stars

Where they do not know where I am, where no one should be.
This is the life in the body: certainty, uncertainty.
I am here, and if they knew, they would not be

What I imagine so easily, the woman a darkness
In the shadow the man above her casts, starlight and arclight
From the window by the bed eclipsing his face from her,

Her legs lifted around him in that delicate poise
Of the almost-come, so when he lowers
His invisible mouth that could be any man's

And takes her breast, her knees stiffen in the same
Upward motion that suddenly and beautifully breaks
This contralto out of her, as the freed light strikes

Her face: that, or some familiar variation. But if they knew
Another darkened body stood on the innocent
Corner of two sidewalks below them listening,

What would they be? I ask myself and know:
Up there in that bedroom I can almost see
With its various reproductions – armoire, nightstand, vanity,

Surrounding its crucially refinished bed –
They would, if they could suddenly know me, stop
Their singular motion in the paralysed reflex of fear,

Afraid, God help me, of nothing, of me,
A human stranger. So knowledge is fear.
I look up at the house spreading its white façade

Streetlight-struck in the blackness of this summer morning,
Five a.m., Vermont, windless and cloudless,
And I see, I want to tell myself simply,

A house. But I know it is no house
I ever lived in. These are the second homes
Of the rich, on a street of stained glass of cupolas

And high balconies where a clichéd lover might declaim
Wherefore? And the answer rise *What light?*
And where lawns of tame maples yield

That storied Vermont sweetness: sap.
I have come here insomniac, waked by a dream
Not frightening, but strange in its inexplicable

And boring complications, the way the mind is,
And I remember the old joke: *The rich*
Are not like us, it goes, to which the answer is

The only one possible: *Right, they have more*
Money. I imagine those two up there, after,
Smoking identical Turkish cigarettes while he tells her

The details of an obscure incident from his childhood.
She nods in the dark and explains. After all,
Her Ph.D. is Viennese and psychological

And ought to do her some good in what she likes
To call her *private life.*
Yes, it is good to lie in the dark and breathe

That alien smoke through bruised lips, good to imagine
The love lives of distant and exotic peoples
In inner-city Detroit or Mississippi

And how, unexamined and mentally unhealthy,
They must hurt each other. And yes, it is good
To stand on the sidewalk hearing it go on and on,

That utterly unknowable woman transcendentally moaning
Out of a life I can only pretend to imagine,
And which I tell myself I could cause

To come to a crashing *coitus interruptus* by a single
Shouted word. Any word would do: *me,*
I could yell, or *here,* or *Detroit,* or *dysfunction,*

It would all be the same word: *fear.*
So words are fear, as long as they let us know
Someone is out there, someone is close by, present

And mysterious in a body that has a familiar shape
But no known face. This is the life
In the body, what we know of each other, the nothing

Names tell us: this is the song
Of the woman touched by the man she thinks
She knows or loves or her life

Would be nothing without
Touching in rooms so dark nobody can say
Who anybody really is, where nobody has

Words songlike enough to touch
The reason I am out here, afraid
Of whoever is up there, lifted

In their Victorian construct
Over the world they speak to without knowing,
Moaning down their wordless and irrefutable explanations,

Giving hands and tongue to name me
Their human groping, making
What even the most petrified among us certainly

Could agree to call *love,* could say
Is good. But now her low voice rises
Toward a classic soprano. I feel its pure

Shudder low in my spine as she tells me
What I translate roughly as *My God*
Someone is doing something right:

And I know I have missed my chance. They are beyond me,
Too far gone for any word
I could shout ever to bring them down.

This is the rapture, these are the sinless
Raised beyond the reach of any voice
Of mine. This is salvation, I am forgiven

My fear and my dreams. I am foretold,
In this flesh that holds me, wherefore
What light (it is the east) grows suddenly unashamed

On the other side of trees that are only
Eclipses of themselves, thrown hard on the edge
Of this world's unnamable laying on of richness.

The Unpoetic

On Being Asked, Whence is the Flower?
after Emerson

It is easy in time to forget
How the depth of dusklight rolls
Over these soybean fields,
Breaker-like, dense, green,

And remember instead the old farmer,
My uncle, who told me *Shit,*
We'll all be finished, boy,
If we don't get rain.

I'm tempted to let that much stand,
As if making two unlike ideas
Fit a single broken breath
Were a big enough thing to do.

But I want it both ways at once.
I want everything. I want to say
I've gone back to that farm
I grew out of years ago, no farmer

By nature. I want to make myself
Visible, standing on the turnrow in light
Slanting through Southern air
So humid I might as well be underwater.

I can't stop this wanting now. That uncle is dead.
Something in his lungs
Ate out his breath, his voice.
You'd think that was final enough.

But light washes over me.
I think *Sea-change*. If I believed
In a spirit separate from the body,
I'd want it to look like this.

It would be pretty to imagine
We went that way, in a tide
Of subaqueous luminescence rising at sunset
Over anybody's best cash crop.

That's all it is, the soybean,
A broad-leaved insignificant-flowered
Concretion of a plant,
Not like the rhodora Emerson talked to

The way I would a lover.
He thought the flower symbolized the soul.
My uncle would have said that was crazy,
But he knew things Emerson never dreamed of.

Look, I make him say, *the soybean stands*
For money, and that's what it gets you
If you live that long, if you believe
In this dirt and sky enough

To sell your soul for rain.
I don't have even that much faith.
All I have is a life, another voice,
Light. And it won't last.

from THE PASSION OF THE RIGHT-ANGLED MAN (1984)

The Age Before Passion

A Vision

In the honey-rich light
Of July Louisiana sun
I see the old
Ford truck bump over the white
Shell road from Hammond

Loaded down
With what sounds like the mutter
Of distant thunderheads,
With a smell dense as ozone
On a night when heat lightning flickers:

A beeyard on wheels,
Stacked high with live
Hives and empties, frames
And foundations, all
The gear you need to give

Bees their care and breeding.
The truck darts in and out
Of shafts of light shot through
Live-oak limbs, light bleeding
Brilliance from the stacked hives, white

And blinding in that air:
Air full of the smell
Of river, the Tangipihoa,
A name obscure
And unpronounceable

To Mississippi boys just over
The line for the first time in their lives,
Two of them, both in khaki,
My uncle and my father.
They are young, their children, their wives

Undreamed of. My father is sixteen.
My uncle, older, drives.
My father's face is grave,
Eyes squinting with wind as he leans
Out the truck window. Behind him, hives

Hum. He hears them,
Turns his head so his ear
Is closer to the slow pulse,
The old dark rhythm
Like heartbeat. The river is near,

And as he turns, a great
White waterbird, egret, rises
From hiding, lifts
Out of oaks. My father's heart
Is quiet. He tries

To follow the egret's flight,
Looks up. I see his head
Tilt against the pure
Glowing white
Of hive behind him, silhouetted,

Eclipsed. If I could see
His face, it would be beautiful
With the peace of his unknowing.
But in the obscurity
Of that brilliance, I only behold

The strong line of jaw, nose,
Hair blown back, blown wild,
Mouth open a little as though
He wants to speak. But no
Words come. I see his dark profile

Light suddenly as the truck
Enters a shadow, shades
Hives from sun. His eyes
Are closed. He looks
Like a man who has just prayed

For something his life is not
Worth a prayer without.
But he has not prayed.
He would not know what
To pray for. He would not

Believe me if I could tell him.
On the road a mile ahead
Is a town. He's going there:
Springfield. It will seem
Like any town he's sweated

To set up a beeyard in.
But that dark-haired fourteen-year-old
Girl across the street
Will watch with strange fascination
As he puts his gloves on, holds

The veil ready. Their eyes will meet.
He will put the beeveil on,
Go to work. The girl is my mother.
She will stand on her side of the street
A long time before she goes home

Wondering why she can hear
Blood beat in her ears so clearly,
What that slow rhythm is
Why birds cry so loud on the river,
Why the sun is so low so early.

Any Time, What May Hit You

The foreman whacks him hard
In the back of the head and calls him
Dumb-ass because he is lost
In the dream of the woman he touched
Last night and lets the milk can slip.
It goes over in a sudden
Explosion of white,
The Holsteins jerk in their stalls,
And the foreman swings
Before the clatter has time to stop.

He lies there a long time after
The foreman stomps out cursing,
Lies flat on his belly
In a puddle of milk, watching one
White rivulet vanish
In the concrete dung trough.
The cattle stop their bucking
And the barn goes still.
The milk, udder-warm, soaks through
His shirt, and he shakes
His head to stop the spinning, feeling
The hand on him sudden
Out of the dark, the wordless
Breath, the lurch
The world took at her touch,
The letting go, the spilling.

The Beating

Everybody knew Clifton Cockerell was not quite bright,
But nobody knew his passion
Till we found him on the playground back of the junior high
Carving names on a tree. His poor secret
Stood no more chance of staying one

Once we had it, than Clifton did of knowing
Why we cared – but we couldn't let it rest,
Till everybody heard it, especially the girl, who was pretty
And though he was some brand of animal. We'd sing
Their names together every chance we got, impressed

With her way of changing colour, like some
Exotic lizard trying to disappear,
And forgot about Clifton pretty much till he came on us
Sudden one afternoon, wrathful and dumb
And swinging a length of cable. It wasn't fear

That defeated us. It was surprise
That it mattered so much what we'd done.
How could we know? He'd been one of us all our lives,
So close it was hard to see how he'd beat us
This once: he was already man enough to think he loved a woman.

So he came down on us sudden, boys,
All of us, and he gave us a taste of the hurt
We'd live to know another way: how love
Can be wrong and still be the only joy
That's real: how, when we come to it,

We stand amazed but take the blow, transfigured, idiot.

Train Wreck, 1890: My Grandmother Lies Down with the Dead

You come to in the past, dark, where the fires still burn
Hot enough in the wreck of the tender to turn iron
Bright, and that red light hovers over the bodies

Heaped just down the embankment – waking, you
Remember only the dream you were having an hour ago,
Asleep on your father's lap in half-dark, dead

Of morning. What was the dream? The porter
Passes quietly in gas-light, sees the right hand
Of the small girl, draped on the fat man's lap, clench.

The fat man is sleeping too, his head lolled
At a broke-neck angle onto the woman's shoulder.
The woman is awake. She takes your hand,

Unrolls the fingers gently. You were holding on
To something in your dream. The porter smiles
At white people's human love, thinks of his own

Granddaughter, tips his cap, goes down
The aisle toward the club car he will never come to.
Coming to, you can only open one eye. Above you

On the slope, coal from the tender smokes thick,
And you think you see men running. Where you are
It is quiet, dark, everything is a long way off

But the dream. You jerk
When the porter slams the door. Your mother
Touches your hair, speaks a word, inaudible, her hand

On your face, in love, in your sleep. She is looking
At your black sweep of hair, delicate twitch
Of eyelids: knows you dream, knows you see

What you will never tell her, something shaken
Out of you by the rattle of the coach, the touch
Of the hand you do not wake to. She leans

Over you, squints at your face, traces,
Not touching skin, the line of your jawbone –
It is not in your dream, the distance of breath

Her fingers are from your face. You will not remember
The hard wonder she stares down at you the moment before
Something breaks deep in the line, the dark you come to

Alone, burned in the shadow of smoke and the lap of the dead
Stranger strange men find you next to, men who lift you,
Look hard in your face, lay you down, believing you

Will never open your eyes in this iron-light of the tender,
Never tell them who, in the black plunge of love,
You belong to again.

from THE ANGELIC ORDERS (1982)

The Naming

In the boys' room at Macon Elementary,
Somebody had written something on the wall in black
Ink, a small neat word I thought
Was a name like other names
Scrawled there, a name like Jack or Buck,
Somebody I hadn't met yet, somebody older,
Maybe already walking the dark
Halls of the high school.

But something inside me knew better
Than to ask about it. Whoever
Belonged to a name like that
Couldn't be spoken of lightly.
He'd drive fast, smoke,
Carry a quick bright knife.

II

They brought the bull over in the back
Of a black truck. I'd never seen one so big.
The heifer in the pen smelled him and lowed
Loud enough to let him
Know it was time. He came down
Quick and ready. From the top
Rail of the corral, I saw him rear,
Saw the red flesh swollen bigger than my arm

Go in. They bellowed and rocked
In the hoof-marked mud of the pen,
And when they were done, my father
Turned and looked at me hard.
I couldn't say what I had seen. But in the spring
They gave the calf my name.

Cow

In the night the belly opened,
The flesh moved in darkness
With the sound of a gate
Swung back for the first time
On rustless hinges.

She lies at the edge of the field
Like something washed up from the sea.
The birds that rise out of her
Are blacker than gulls.

Hanging Fire

Little Willy's daddy used to hang him
Up in a croker sack over a slow fire
When he was peeved. He'd throw
Wet leaves on the flames till the smoke came thick,
Then get the sack swinging – he didn't want
To burn the boy, just make him think –
And as Willy swung, his daddy would swing
A piece of one-by-two at him, aiming for the rump
Which sometimes he didn't hit quite right,
It being neither here nor there.

Every time Willy came out of the sack, he came out black
With soot, black with bruises, blackhearted,
Wouldn't talk for days. I couldn't tell him
Willy, it's wrong, you feeling that way
Like his mother did when he went back to the house.
I couldn't say anything to him. I'd just watch
That woman scrub for hours at his stubborn body,
Her black arms sweating, swearing as she scrubbed
That if it was the last thing she ever did
On this good earth, she'd make him shine.

Night Burning

In the night meadow, grassfire burns
My eyes till only the shadows
Are good to look on. It takes
Care to make a fire that touches
Only what you want touched.
It takes a life of burning
And knowing what to burn.

One night when I was a child
I woke to the changing
Light of pasture fire. I turned
To the window, saw
Lines of flame sweep
My father's dark fields.
I thought *What if he loses it,*
What if it breaks away,
What if everything burns?

I saw my hands catch fire,
I touched the sheets, the quilts,
Let go of it, let it rise
Into the rafters until
The black roof split
And the October sky
Opened to nothing I could name,

And in that moment of joy
When I did not know who I was
I saw my father walking
Over the fields, the blinding
Torch in his hand falling,
Touching, rising – the earth
Beneath him turning
Dark and light.

Eclipse

For Mary Helen Jackson Hummer
1885 – 1979

This moment was foretold to me: the face
Of the moon goes dim, curdled like milk laced with vinegar,
As the night-drunk owl I answered for hours falls
Silent suddenly. And now I am left with nothing
But my own prophesies to tell me what is to come:

Shadow of the earth, darkness hidden in darkness,
Song of a night-bird caught in its own echo –
Things I have always known, just as I always
Know each moment of my own life only the moment before
It fades in its own incalculable shadow.

Where You Go When She Sleeps

What is it when a woman sleeps, her head bright
In your lap, in your hands, her breath easy now as though it had never been
Anything else, and you know she is dreaming, her eyelids
Jerk, but she is not troubled, it is a dream
That does not include you, but you are not troubled either,
It is too good to hold her while she sleeps, her hair falling
Richly on your hands, shining like metal, a colour
That when you think of it you cannot name, as though it has just
Come into existence, dragging you into the world in the wake
Of its creation, out of whatever vacuum you were in before,
And you are like the boy you heard of once who fell
Into a silo full of oats, the silo emptying from below, oats
At the top swirling in a gold whirlpool, a bright eddy of grain, the boy,
You imagine, leaning over the edge to see it, the noon sun breaking
Into the centre of the circle he watches, hot on his back, burning,
And he forgets his father's warning, stands on the edge, looks down,
The grain spinning, dizzy, and when he falls his arms go out, too thin
For wings, and he hears his father's cry somewhere, but he is gone

Already, down in a gold sea, spun deep in the heart of the silo,
And when they find him, his mouth, his throat, his lungs
Full of the gold that took him, he lies still, not seeing the world
Through his body but through the deep rush of the grain
Where he has gone and can never come back, though they drag him
Out, his father's tears bright on both their faces, the farmhands
Standing by blank and amazed – you touch that unnameable
Colour in her hair and you are gone into what is not fear or joy
But a whirling of sunlight and water and air full of shining dust
That takes you, a dream that is not of you but will let you
Into itself if you love enough, and will not, will never let you go.

Selected Long Poems
and Sequences
1978-2001

Carrier (1978)

for my father

WITHOUT GUILT, THE RURAL CARRIER READS A POSTCARD

They're fair game. Anyone who would write
Anything important on the back of one is a fool.
I saw one once that said, *Dear Mama: Hope you are physical.*
Also mental. Saw the reply: *I'm all right,*
Son, just the same. I lost some sleep that night
Thinking. That was years ago. Now all
I do is nod when I read them. But I read them all.
You can't make a secret of what's in plain sight.

I had an old woman on the route once who could get
Whole letters on them. Long ones. Wrote so small
I had to squint in strong sunlight to read it.
Wrote everywhere, sideways, upside-down, diagonal.
Never had much to say. But what she said
I turned sideways, upside-down, and by God read.

THE RURAL CARRIER DELIVERS A C.O.D. PACKAGE
TO A BLIND PATRON

She says I'm honest. She says she knows I can count.
So she gives me a fifty and trusts me for the change.
A thin string runs from her doorknob out
To the mailbox. She never lets it go. We exchange
Bills, coins, papers. She signs her name
Left-handed, holding on with her right.
She says she knows I understand. I say the same
Thing I always say: *It's all right, ma'am. It's all right.*

It's a package from Sears, Roebuck. An electric blanket.
Says she needs it these cold nights. She sleeps alone.
It's all right, though. Says she knows that house. She can get
Anything she wants. There's nothing she can't lay her hand on.
She props the box on one hip and follows that string
Back, after reaching to pat my arm and patting nothing.

79

The Rural Carrier Admires Neil Varner's
Brand New Convertible

On Main Street, right in front of the Ford place,
Neil Varner's convertible sits, as well as it can
With no front wheels, hardly any front end,
The engine in the front seat, and in the space
Where it should be, crushed metal, not an inch
Left smooth, that used to be hood, grill, and bumper.
The windshield's gone. There's dried blood everywhere.
But they say he walked away drunk, without even a scratch.

Look in the back seat, somebody says. I look.
There's nearly half a cow back there, the butt end,
Cut off neat above the legs and nestled in
The black vinyl cushion. Black Angus. Black against black.
They say he was doing ninety when he hit her.
They're still looking for the head. It could be anywhere.

The Rural Carrier Resists Temptation

Angie Lloyd, like something slipped loose from heaven,
She's so good looking, comes down from her house trailer wanting
To buy a book of stamps. I'm ready with it when
She gets to me. Every Monday morning
We meet like this. It's a hell of a way to live,
A hell of a thing to live with. She reaches in
The car window, holds out a five. I give
Her what she needs, lay it on the soft white skin

Of her upturned palm. Then I'm ready to make her
Change. I let her have it, slow but right.
She walks away satisfied. I watch her out of sight
Wondering if there's anything she can't shake.
But then I think, I've gone this far
With her. Things could be worse than they are.

THE RURAL CARRIER DISCOVERS THAT LOVE IS EVERYWHERE

A registered letter for the Jensens. I walk down their drive
Through the gate of their thick-hedged yard, and by God there they are,
On a blanket in the grass, asleep, buck-naked, honeymooners
Not married a month. I smile, turn to leave,
But can't help looking back. They're a pretty sight,
Both of them, tangled up in each other, easy in their skin –
It's their own front yard, after all, perfectly closed in
By privet hedge and country. Maybe they were up all night.

I want to believe they'd do that, not thinking of me
Or anyone but themselves, alone in the world
Of the yard with its clipped grass and fresh-picked fruit trees.
Whatever this letter says can wait. To hell with the mail.
I slip through the gate, silent as I came, and leave them
Alone. There's no one they need to hear from.

LOOKING IN THE REAR-VIEW MIRROR, THE RURAL CARRIER THINKS
HE CATCHES A GLIMPSE OF THE ANGEL OF DEATH HANGING OVER
GEORGE GILLESPIE'S MAILBOX

A clear day, not even a crow in the air
Over George Gillespie's as I put the mail
In his box. The usual stuff, except for the one bill,
The one he's been waiting for, from the funeral parlour.
He's asked about it twice. The first time was the day
After his wife was buried. He came to the road
When he saw my car. Asked if I had it. Said he owed
Somebody something. Said he was ready to pay.

The second time was some days later. He just stood there,
And when I shook my head, he walked off, nodding.
I haven't seen him since, though every morning
When I come by, his curtains tremble. He knows I'm here.
He knows my moves, how I hang out my window to slip
Something in his box. He knows how to add things up.

THE RURAL CARRIER SEES JERNIGAN'S FIELD HAND EATEN

In the middle of Jernigan's wheatfield, I saw something wrong:
A combine driving itself. I thought I was dreaming
Till I stopped the car and looked again. It was going along
By itself, all right. No driver. Than I heard the screaming,
And saw him on the front, trying to climb up the reel.
I ran, but he was a hundred yards away.
He rose, then went down. Running, I could feel
The scream in my own throat as he hit the hay

That was riding over the cutter-bar into the auger.
Later they said he must have been trying to unclog it,
Left it running while he worked, and it slipped into gear.
All I know is, when I saw him hit,
I didn't stop running. But a fine
Spray of blood blew out of the back of the machine.

THE RURAL CARRIER STOPS TO KILL A NINE-FOOT COTTONMOUTH

Lord God, I saw the son-of-a-bitch uncoil
In the road ahead of me, uncoil and squirm
For the ditch, squirm a hell of a long time.
Missed him with the car. When I got back to him, he was all
But gone, nothing left on the road but the tip-end
Of his tail, and that disappearing into Johnson grass.
I leaned over the ditch and saw him, balled up now, hiss.
I aimed for the mouth and shot him. And shot him again.

Then I got a good strong stick and dragged him out.
He was long and evil, thick as the top of my arm.
There are things in this world a man can't look at without
Wanting to kill. Don't ask me why. I was calm
Enough, I though. But I felt my spine
Squirm suddenly. I admit it. It was mine.

A Crazy Girl Brings the Rural Carrier a Dime

Every day she meets me at the mailbox, holding
Her hand out. It's not the mail she wants.
I've tried to give it to her, but she won't
Take it – just stretches her arm toward me, unfolding
Her fingers from the palm. And there's the dime.
She wants me to have it. I ask her *What do you need?*
She won't answer. She reaches toward me, shaking her head
Like there's something we both know. Time after time

I've shrugged my shoulders at her and driven on.
A ten-cent stamp, a cigarette – nothing satisfies her.
Every day, no matter what, she's there.
Christ, the way she looks, waiting for me in the rain!
Once I thought she followed me home. I started
To take her in my arms, hold her: *Is this what you wanted?*

A Poem for my Father, Written in the City

My father's hills buried under frost,
My father's trees breaking under ice
The backs of his cattle covered with wind –
In the sound of sleet, the breath of my father's country

Reveals itself in sleep, in the hiss of sleet on water,
The whisper that rises out of cattails constantly growing
Darker with winter, transfigured now at the edge
Of the pond, where the tracks of cattle harden.

It is only in winter that I remember this:
The land bent with the weight of a lifetime of ice.
But nothing is ever lost. I think of it suddenly now

When I hear, like something terribly distant, the sleet
Vanishing into gutters: and God knows I am still
A child, asleep, and I have not got beyond the earth.

Bluegrass Wasteland (1989)

With apologies
To Bob Bernard and Bob Cantwell

And to Johnny
the mandolin player
for the Flat Mountain Boys
of Stillwater, Oklahoma
who squinted down from the bandstand
at the Wild Willy's bar crowd
and muttered into the microphone
Ain't nothing out there, friends,
But a bluegrass wasteland.

I

In Louisiana summer, hurricanes lift
Their unpersonifiable vastnesses out of the Gulf of Mexico
And hammer into the mainland, looking for no one.

The boy sits in a tall chair staring out a plate-glass storm door
Onto the brick patio where rain shivers canna leaves to pulp.
A book lies open in his lap, a cheap old edition

Of Jules Verne's 20,000 Leagues Under the Sea.
From it an odour rises of disuse and loneliness,
Of the sweat of librarians and antiseptic dust.

He found it on a high shelf of the local parish library
Where nobody had touched it in years, no names on its card,
And brought it to his grandmother's house to sit reading alone

Of the madness of Captain Nemo. The book's spine creaks
As the storm takes shape over the Gulf. Outside the round
Crystal window of the Nautilus, unimaginable creatures move.

When the boy grow up, he will remember only vaguely
The submarine's interior, the characters' names, the action:
But the lonely crazy old man who played the pipe organ deep undersea

Will have a definite face in his mind, a distinct voice.
And he will remember the storm, how the earth-coloured urns
Planted with succulents on the patio keep blurring in rain.

Why should any of this seem sad? In some future, it will all assume
The lineaments of high tragedy, the captain and his beautiful
Miraculous home-made machine, the broken leaves on the bricks,

The cheap iron-black patio furniture quicksilvered with storm.
Where will it all be going? It is going down,
Derelict wreckage, sinking, spun

In the vortex of hurricane. Now, as he looks through the glass,
It becomes a dull ache of excitement he will one day think he understands
Is sexual. But even that will be wrong, only a word that means

As much as Mozart would mean if you heard that music played
From deep underwater while you floated in a lifeboat
Terrified, praying for rescue, singled out, cannibal.

II

We choose how to begin. We choose touch
In a dark room, alone. We choose nakedness
Come by the hard way, and slow.

There is the deliberate awkwardness
Of clothes, the motion, the time it takes
To take them off,

Not the way we like to imagine them
Simply disappearing in a cinematic dissolve:
They cling. They demand

To be consciously removed.
The pale slow uplift of pullover wool
Holds on to the woman's breasts.

Even in this dark, the man sees them rise,
Fall, released. Now there should be
Some beautiful image coming

Out of all this circumstance,
Out of their being here, out of their bodies,
But it would be a lie to say

Whiteness, calyx, lip
Of snow, lip of blood.
If there is going to be suffering

There must be an authority for pain.
Touch me is all she can tell him.
There is no true or adequate story.

III

Outside, moonlight calcifies the asphalt
And two station wagons parked in the shadow
Of a gut-rotted crab-apple tree. Even here, where a side street

Arcs by a parking lot, if you want pure nature, all you have to do
Is look straight up. No matter what's on the moon, what's in the air,
That ought to be enough for anyone.

A convertible drifts by, discoloured by moonlight and arclight,
Roof up, window rolled down a crack, bluegrass on the radio –
Blue moon of Kentucky, keep on shining –

And nobody thinks a thing about it,
Nobody connects it to anything, until
In the dark office, the man and woman prepare

To begin making love. Later, they will both remember it
Absurd and sad – in an office, in a room without a bed,
Silhouettes of typewriters, telephones, file cabinets

Hard-edged in what passes for that room's darkness,
Somebody's report half-written and glowing
On the desktop like moon-suffused snowlight –

But neither will way it to the other, ever.
You could name everything here – *desk lamp, ledger,*
Pocketbook, car key, pavement, crabapple, moon –

And never be outside nature, never even begin
To get beyond the clear hard perfection
Passion flowers into from its root word *pain.*

They don't understand. They touch and go on touching.
In the dark, they have voices, wordless but real.
They touch and the voices begin: touch, and begin again.

IV

Now things get dangerous. Consciousness floats free.
Shaken loose from first person, the voice can say anything.
All sorts of pernicious illusions come to mind:

The cinematic illusion, say, where the language rises
Against the reader's imagination like images on film –
Or is it images on a screen? – and assumes that authority

Of instantaneous occurrence, *comme ça:*
Frame: through a cyclone fence, two Ford station wagons
In soft focus first behind the wire's diamond grid,

Then full focus as the fence wire fuzzes and fades.
There must be some significance in this image,
The reader, now viewer, assumes, since it stays so long onscreen.

The cars have an atmosphere of melancholy abandonment,
Left sitting all this time in the parking lot of a drab brick building
Which looks like the headquarters of some borderline business,

An insurance office, a chiropractor's, a miserable savings and loan.
And there may be something symbolic about the fence,
Holding in, as it did at first, the quintessential

American domestic automobile: indicating,
Perhaps, the confinement of contemporary marriage?
But this is all critical speculation, as the viewer is reminded

When the camera, without moving, drops
A frost-rotted crabapple from a high branch of the dark old tree
The cars sit under. It falls dead centre

On a hood, and the viewer becomes
Listener: This film has sound, you realize.
Whang, the apple goes. Or does the hood go *thud?*

Whichever, the apple bounces now in artsy slow motion
And the viewer notices the stain. Always the stain.
This is a different illusion, *the oracular illusion,*

As possible as any other. No accident
The one at Delphi was only a voice,
Untrustworthy, never accountable, never *I.*

    v

Comme ça: *His grandmother used to say that.*
She got it from the Cajuns she grew up with
In South Louisiana, and for her it meant

Do it this way – *not a good translation,*
But he knew what she was saying. Eat your gumbo,
She'd tell him. Comme ça.

And she'd play-eat hers with a fork.
It was French, but it wasn't intellectual.
It was a joke. It was technique. It was rhetoric insofar

As it was persuasion. It worked.
Shrimp, crab, oyster:
He was landlocked, he didn't like those words.

They made him remember feelers and eyes and fish-stink cooking.
But sitting at the old walnut table
In her kitchen, he's watch her, he'd giggle,

He'd eat. Out through the casement window, the camellia
Incandesced in March Louisiana sun,
And the live oaks dropped their old moss-strokes

From limb to limb to the ground.
We like to talk about remembering,
How everything assumes

Clarity at memory's centre, no matter
That it fades to strange around the edges
Like the clichéd fly hung in nebulous amber:

Comme ça, *said his grandmother.*
She dipped her fork in his bowl, pretended to eat, and he
Ate truly: and though it was easier to swallow

While she did that, he still didn't like it.
It didn't seem fair to have to eat strange food
Just because he wasn't at home, just because the air

Through the window was dense with what he did not know
Was simple humidity. He could only see
It made everything different, an unfamiliar

Soup of a world. In his bowl, there were small sea creatures
He didn't want to think about, didn't want inside his body.
They reminded him of great depths, of sub-aqueous darknesses.

Comme ça, *his grandmother said, waving her fork.*
Do it this way. Do it this way.
And the red claw of camellia swam under fathoms of light.

While that was happening, the woman wrestles
Her pale blue pullover off, drops it on the carpet.
She shrugs out of her brassiere, stands in a shaft of murky light

That comes down from the room's one small high window.
Her breasts are of medium size and have the slight sag
That reflects her middle age and signifies her children.

Her nipples are heavy and half-stiff, beginning now
To lift from large aureoles of indistinct roundness,
Permanently goosefleshed. *This is the clinical illusion.*

The man, in spite of any troubling questions
About time and verb tense and morality, is sitting in front of her.
He has found an honest straight-backed wheel-less chair –

In that room full of objects designed for maximum efficiency
It seems old-fashioned, a miracle of domesticity –
And he sits fully clothed looking up at her.

His lips part. Will he speak? What will he say?
Language is magic, a technique, one
Which is born of desire, and which assures desire

Its being by means born of desire?
Who would he have to be to say such a thing?
Not who he is, not anybody he knows.

He holds out both hands like a deaf-mute signing,
Moves his palms on her breasts in gentle circles.
She understands. She steps closer to him

And he takes her left nipple into his mouth.
His tongue moves, and she speaks, she moans, and it means
Yes. Do it that way. Do it this way.

Always this sense that something is missing, always
This feeling there is something to be looked for
Blind, the way the newborn nuzzles for the mother's breast

And sucks that strange food down: this is the life in the body.
In December moonlight, a convertible circles the building,
Teenaged boys clichéd for love, thirsty. In the front seat,

One puts his hand in a sack, passes out tall cans of beer.
Aluminium shines under arclight, and the sudden foam
Hisses out of shaken cans onto their hands in the intervening darkness.

This is an image of masturbation or an image of the sea
Throwing itself with painless obsession
Against jagged and unyielding shorelines, this is an image of the seed

Of hyperbole or epic simile ready to uncoil
Out of the eight-cylinder rhythm of home-bored and –modified engines
And the hard certainty of horniness which is nothing but the root

Of the will to romance and the will to war and the will
To settle down and raise children quietly in the suburbs
After they appear suddenly in a life

Spent driving and drinking through streets at night
In a town you never asked to be born in, never liked the name of,
Never understood was the only town you could ever love

Because it prints itself hard-edged against the foam you turn into
While you beat yourself against it for years
Trying to wear it down, wear it away:

But it compensates perfectly, it accommodates itself
With quiet and infuriating unconsciousness to everything you do,
Takes the shape of your body, accepts your obsession

Without trouble or recognition, takes on your face
Easily, since you belonged to it in the first place
And it could not have been otherwise and can never be otherwise

No matter how fast and hard you drive
Dreaming of the bodies of teenaged girls who live
In houses so far from you

The machine that bears you would rust apart beneath you
Before you had travelled an nth part of the distance:
Your body would sink in the dust of its own going down.

VIII

The second person illusion, *the intimate illusion,*
The illusion that drags you in.
You didn't want to be here. But nobody else did either,

And everybody has to be somewhere.
So this is Mt. Vernon, Ohio, and you are a stranger
In the sudden particularity of this secondary illusion, *fact.*

How real is it going to be, you want to know?
The incidents of this illusion are purely a fiction. The literal facts
Are chiefly connected with the natural and artificial

Objects and customs of the inhabitants. Which is to say, everything.
That's how the voice protects itself, that's how it lies to confuse
Your sense of who you are and where you are, that's how it makes you

Believe in the concrete reality of what is after all pure voice:
Claiming to remind you that none of this is real,
It lets you know in passing and underhandedly

That after all it *is,* and leaves you
To sort it out for yourself. In moonlight, Mt. Vernon, Ohio,
Is equivocal anyway, a town of antebellum houses and brick streets

And honky-tonks where the inhabitants shoot pool quietly.
They have their own objects and customs, these good Americans
Who never give a second thought to life in the heartland.

They work all week and on the weekends they drink, seldom get drunk,
And on Sunday they go to church in the morning, watch football all afternoon.
That's easy to say, and the voice is ashamed of itself

For the distance it can't help keeping from the inarticulate mystery
Of every human life. But what, after all, *are* the facts?
Somewhere in town, a husband and wife, pleasantly sleepy

From drinking a couple of beers while watching a TV movie,
Go to the bedroom, tune in a country-western station on the clock radio,
Make love satisfactorily but without great intensity,

Fall asleep. And that ought to be the whole story.
But in the middle of the night, one of them wakes up
To the sound of static: wakes with the weight of the body

Of a husband or wife heavy across his or her thighs,
Blood cut off: the flesh-tingle and the static
One thing, a voice without words, without human presence,

Omnipotent as death or human fate, which are one in the same –
And the one who wakes (the man or the woman? does it matter?) wants
To scream, it is so nightmarish to be awake in this half-dead body,

In this bedroom with another who is a sleeping stranger, unable to move,
Unable to reach the radio switch and stop that sound
Leaking from God knows where (out of the earth's

Magnetic field? out of the stars?) into the bedroom where the two of them lie
And have lied to each other and go on lying to themselves
In everything simple, in saying each other's names,

In saying *love* or *breakfast,* all that matters and does not matter,
And is nothing but the ongoing nothing
That wakes in the dark and hears that voice the radio makes

Present and out of reach, which is the voice
You can hear all over Mt. Vernon, Ohio, in the moonlight
If you are the *you* who has given yourself up

To this particular illusion. It is as if
The moonlight itself is hissing on the bricks
Of streets and houses, the godvoice behind everything.

IX

At a party once, the woman tried to explain
A feeling she sometimes had that everything was falling apart.
"You mean spiritually, morally?" somebody asked. No:

She meant physically, and she meant *everything.*
She was a little drunk, and so were the others,
So explaining was hard. Finally somebody said,

"Yeah, the bomb," as if that settled the question.
Drinking, the woman considered: Maybe it *was* the bomb,
But right away she knew that was wrong. She had an image

Of how it would be when the bomb went off,
A soundless flash of angelic white, then blindness, burning.
This was different. This happened slowly, from within.

It made a sound like bricks scraping over bricks,
Like an engine throwing a rod, like somebody coughing up phlegm.
She had a feeling, though she did not know where it came from,

There was nothing new about it. She had a feeling
That sound had been around forever,
People had always heard it

But pretended not to, like now. "Put on some music," somebody said.
No, she wanted to tell them, *wait, listen –*
But too late. The stereo arm came down.

In the dark, in the office, in the straight-backed chair
The man lets the woman's nipple go, looks up.
Her head is tilted toward him, her long hair falls

Forward and down around her face, touches his.
Her hands cradle his head. One cups each ear gently.
The hears the small echo of air in the shells of her hands,

Hears the tick of her wristwatch, her breath, her heart,
A car with a bad muffler revving by in the street.
In that whole hierarchy of sounds, there is nothing he understands.

The stereo played Bill Monroe: "Blue Moon of Kentucky."
"Yeah," somebody said, "the High Lonesome Sound,"
And the host and hostess, drunk, leaned on each other, waltzing.

In the music, the high-pitched nervous plink of mandolin
Worried the stern three-quarter-time guitar,
A counterpoint emblematic of some old sorrow.

She looked at her husband. He sat across the table
Nursing a long beer, ready to go home.
And sometimes, those nights, she would look out the kitchen window

While the kids did homework in the other room or watched TV,
And imagine that once the whole surface of things ground itself away
There would be something underneath it, another world, angels, or light,

And she thought it would be worth it then, even if everybody died:
Just an instant of transparency. She touches the man's face.
He takes her breast again. It is some old reflex

Forgotten since infancy. He remembers how his wife would rub her nipple
On their newborn son's cheek to remind him how to nurse.
He remembers the sound of nursing, the sound of crying,

Remembers the high clear tenor voice on the radio –
Blue moon of Kentucky, keep on shining –
Remembers the circle of moon turning dark, turning light.

x

She is now so responsive to his kissing her breasts
That he can give her a climax in that way.
He still finds it astonishing, miraculous, a gift

From the god of biology. As if the rest of it weren't enough,
Just when the body seems limited, insufficient: this.
Just when there needs to be more to touch, more parts of the body made

To correspond to touch, the body answers
Through surrender to this desire,
To this need that calls itself love.

So passion is a transfiguring force, something beyond
Delight and pain: beatitude?
But passion means pain, a fact which we forget.

Which suffering comes next? Perhaps the hands
Will turn entirely sexual under this heat,
Perhaps touching hands will be all it will take.

And then perhaps the skin of the whole body.
Think of that: The lover's touch anywhere at all,
Or the touch of clothing, the simple touch of air,

Might be enough. And beyond that? The blood, the lungs?
So that one's very being, heartbeat and breath,
Night turn to a single lifelong climax, which we would not call

Sex any longer, but mystical pain, in which we would lose
Awareness of that which suffers, in which we would come,
Literally, at last, to gnosis?

It is a voice. It has a source.
He kisses her breasts, he touches her nipples with his tongue
And hears Jesus cry out on the cross.

Which melodramatic heresy is this? Does it have a name?
Call it the heretic illusion if you have to call it:
When it comes to you, it is absolute authority, pure justification.

XI

On the outskirts of Mt. Vernon, Ohio, the voice assumes
The foursquare shape of a cinder-block honky-tonk.
Inside, musicians tune instruments, warm up, run a sound check.

It's still a while until show time. Nobody's in the bar
Except the bartender, two barmaids, and one hard-core
Old drunk, a constant customer. But the musicians are antsy,

Not nervous, exactly, but anxious, ready.
They sit at a small table in front of the bandstand. One
Has a mandolin, one a banjo, one a fiddle, one a guitar,

And they start to play an old hornpipe they won't do on-stage,
Simple but intricate, unamplified, no good to two-step to.
Plainness, although simple, is not what I mean by simplicity.

Simplicity is a clean, direct expression of that essential
Quality of the thing which is the nature of the thing itself.
They play this for themselves, they play it for no one.

The drunk at the bar turns around to watch them.
From where he sits, he can see the soft shine
Of bar lights on the mandolin's mother-of-pearl.

The voice might have him think anything now –
His mother, a lover, a good time in another town –
And say it is the music that guides his remembering,

That it makes him suddenly happy or sad or angry or dissatisfied:
But this wouldn't do justice to the momentum of the inarticulate
Life that brings him here night after night

To drink cheap bourbon and purposely thing about nothing.
There is a beauty in thinking nothing. It is more than simple-minded.
The musicians are thinking nothing. The fiddle player's eyes

Close as he gives his small life up to the life
Of Vassar Clements or Tommy Jarrell, to every hero of the fiddle
Whose wisdom is greater than his or any singular mind's.

The banjo player turns his hands into patterns
Evolved by generations of hands frailing the patterned
Necks of banjos. If he thinks, he drops the rhythm.

The drunk touches his glass. He is one of a long line
Of drunks. He can lose himself in tradition.
Later the band will play other, louder music

On-stage, and the bar will fill
With smoke and talk and the sexual odour of sweat,
And lovers will give up their lives

To the form of being lovers, and barmaids to the form
Of slapping the forms of the hands of solitary men
Pinching the lovely forms of buttocks drifting by.

But for now what they do they do quietly, in the spirit
Of meditation or prayer or gentle foreplay, their feet
Together tapping time's formality on the hardwood dance floor.

XII

Isn't it luminosity we are after?
Isn't it the high old style?
But the irony is, just at the critical juncture

She has to lower herself.
She stands in front of him, his right leg between her legs.
A small adjustment of her skirt lets her bare skin touch his pants.

She eases herself down. She feels him change
From her left breast to her right. She straddles him, she rocks, moans.
All utterance cherishes an object outside itself,

All words refer us to the world.
But who understands how? Is this *the objective illusion?*
Dull questions, in the face of which she clamps

Her legs around his leg and rises
To a more than rhetorical climax,
A tension easily aroused and satisfied,

Real enough, but not enough, a stopping point
On the way to the ultimate argument.
She holds his head in the dark between her hands,

Intuits, the way bodies can, the distance between
Her palms. It is so small
She suddenly wants to weep with pity and fear

At what that space contains.
She pulls him from her breast, tilts his face toward her.
All around them, the ominous

Shapes of the workplace gather.
She can see his face. She cannot see his face.
She wants to tell him something, but in her own head

The words sound sentimental, melodramatic, dangerous.
Their definitions have a sudden terrible clarity.
She kisses him, mouth open. She gives him her tongue.

Nothing but confusion has ever come
From the effort to fix the male/female boundary.
The opaque attitude proves useful for both.

Clarity? The moon: the arclight
Hung like its brighter reflection
High in the parking lot:

Milk-blue light that filters down
Through the small, high office window.
That's all clear enough,

Not man or woman or human but the world.
But in the opaque dark of the body,
Where we find ourselves and our story,

Such as it is, the slow old blood does its work.
She unbuttons his shirt, lays her hands
Against his chest, feels

His heart utter its simple repetitious word.
It refers to her. It refers her to herself.
That's what she'd doing here, that's why her tongue

Moves itself in his mouth, that's why the dark
It moves in refuses to lighten to the syllable
That rises blind in the body: *name, name, name.*

XIII

Are you starting to get a feel for how the voice
Echoes? How *echo* here means motion in space *and* time?
It travels the way a lover's mumbled word crawls the arc

Of a domed building in India, a hundred yards along the wall
To the beloved, while nobody standing in the middle overhears a thing –
Or like the melodramatic stage whisper a woman hallucinates

In a low-budget movie when the director wants it understood
She's remembering something somebody said years ago.
The theory is, such motion is transcendence and thus salvation.

That's how it is with voices. The man, the voice can say,
Remembers, hears, anything at all the moment the woman lays
The satin whisper of her panties against his leg:

He embodies, for instance, in an instantaneous flash of imagistic recall,
The classroom at a state university twenty years ago,
A decrepit humanities building, a day in late September,

Hot Indian summer, all the windows open,
Everyone in the class half asleep in that late afternoon,
While the teacher, a smartass graduate assistant,

Shows off what he knows about oracles.
Croesus, king of the Lydians, on the eve of going to war,
Inquired of the Delphic Oracle what the outcome would be,

And was told A great kingdom will fall, *which he did not take to mean*
His own. That's an old story, written somewhere in chapter one
Of the history of irony. Every college freshman learns it

Who stays awake in World Civilization 1-A.
The original Delphi was dedicated not
To the cult of Apollo, but to a female

Subterranean power, that of the great snake Delphyne,
Whose name conceals an archaic word for the womb.
Oracles are generally associated with the underworld,

And the oracle of Delphi was older than Apollo.
Can he really remember all that at such a moment?
Say *yes* – he can remember that and more:

The particular buzz of a particular fly twenty years dead,
One of a near-infinite line of flies stretching back
Into the world's impenetrable prehistory further even than Delphyne,

Which flew into the stultified air of that classroom,
Black and heavy and itself half asleep or half dead
With the winter that the specialized sensitivity

Of its highly evolved body to certain death
Had to know was coming, Indian summer or no Indian summer:
His hand reaching up in a graceful clever motion

To snatch the fly alive out of the air
And contain the dull confusion of its buzzing
In a fly-sized flesh-hollow (he learned this trick

From his cousin on the farm, how easy it is
To catch flies in the air where they can't control
Even the tininess of their own momentum), and holding it, realizing

The power of life and death. The odds were fifty-fifty:
Kill it, let it go. Now let the oracle speak,
The oracle of flies, which this fly doubtless

Neglected to consult, or, if it did,
Received advice misleading, ambiguous, and dangerous.
If I kill this fly, he thought, *a great kingdom will fall.*

And now, of course, the voice is going to tell you
That no matter how detailed this memory is so far,
The man cannot for the life of him be sure

What came next. He can easily imagine that he opened
His hand in godlike mercy, or with equal ease that he flipped it
Floorward with a godlike wrist-snap of vengeance.

What does it matter? The fly died anyway.
The lesson? The future is certain. It's the past
We can't be sure of.

The woman moans, stiffens, coming.
O voice, O cheap and easy guide
To the inevitable, we bring you

Offerings, we pray you will explain
How the strange knotted taste of a nipple of flesh
Lives, and has its life in another life.

His hands are under her skirt. He touches nylon satin,
Touches skin. He knows muscle and bone, the highly evolved
And specialized body, come

Out of how many identical moments of the underworld
We call *time,* brought by how many accidental godlike touches
To this particular echo of *ekstasis?*

XIV

Where are we now? Have we even begun? The voice
Wonders at itself, moves in wonder at the way
It shapes the word it understands as love, moves to tell us

Mt. Vernon, Ohio, is a place of various edges:
Some shopping malls, some farms and orchards,
Some suburbs, some the local equivalent of slums,

But the churches all want to sit close to the centre, where
They can build bell towers to toll out tunes territorial
As birdsong over the town square park. From here,

In the heart of *the blank verse illusion,* we can scan
Town square glowing in the hot illumination
Of floodlights the city fathers long ago

Saw the necessity of, to hold down sex
And violence – can see it from, as it were, a great height.
Again the high style. It would be easy now

To say this is Mt. Vernon's empty centre,
This square, these sacred benches and trees
And sad wedding-cake fountain of whitewashed iron

Pissing up four inadequate streamlets from edges to heart –
Easy, but the voice resists. Sometimes even irony
Can be too simple. Look again. You forgot to see

The statue, the centre of the centre.
Everything else is submission to the fractured vision
Of the human world, which isolates everything you do –

103

Eating, dressing, earning money, making love –
And what is beyond? How can it all go on?
Don't you understand yet? This is the voice

Of desperation, looking for a method
To speak of these things without alienation, without scorn.
At the centre of town square, as we see from our lonely height,

Is a statue, ordinary in material, subject, style:
Grey stone, a Civil War soldier abstract as Jesus,
Brother to a thousand others all over the country, North and South alike,

Its four-faced pedestal carved to quantify
History and passion, to name names but to tell no story.
In the centre of Mt. Vernon, Ohio, it lifts a countervoice:

East face:

ERECTED BY THE MOUNT VERNON
LADIES' MONUMENT ASSOCIATION
JULY 4, A.D. 1877

North face:

IN HONOR
OF THE VICTORIES
AND OF THE TRIUMPH
OF THE NATIONAL ARMS
IN THE WAR OF THE
GREAT REBELLION
1861-5
AND IN MEMORY
OF THE
NOBLE SONS OF KNOX COUNTY, OHIO,
WHO FOUGHT AND WHO FELL
IN THAT CONFLICT

West face:

South face:

It is the beaten countervoice of the human life
Of men and women in the United States of North America
And everything that means, the clichés and black holes

Of history and social theory, Manifest Destiny's urban sprawl
Gouged into stone, its line breaks predetermined
Not by prosody's arbitration but by the definite physical size

Of a six-ton chunk of granite bought and paid for
By charitable ministrations performed in the august name
Of the Mt. Vernon Ladies' Monument Association,

Its phrasing institutional and unconsciously sexual
As the soft white hands of Knox County wives knitting booties
To sell in service of mounting their heroic erection

In the centre of Mt. Vernon, under the tritely phallic shadows
Of steeples, where now from the voice's unconscionable height,
We watch love-cars circle in arclight, drawn predictably as moths

To the flamelike stone soldier, whose face is so abstractly human
It is everyone's: and the boys in the white convertible forget
Their great rebellion as they drive, watching the shadowed park

For predestined women who exist nowhere except
In the conventional mind we all share, which insists this circling
Go on and on creating the life of what we call a nation, forever one:

Countervoice, reactionary echo thrown against storefronts, church doors,
Walls of houses where the righteous married carry on
Their fated and mythic domesticity:

Rhetoric thrown against the unyielding cold
Surface of statue-pedestal, circumventing every word
Of cynicism, irony, criticism, scorn, doubt,

Denying the existence of illusion, denying error and sin,
Obliterating the private life except as it gives itself up
Pro patria: voice and countervoice

Collide, cancel out, resurrect themselves,
Renew each other, wrestle toward death, desire each other
While the centre of town trembles its silent detonation.

   xv

Above it all, over cartops and rooftops and treetops,
In that dark and ambiguous one between biosphere and vacuum,
Moonlight shatters on an arctic cloud-mass blown

Due south under a sudden cold front filled with snow.
If we could define the physical world, if we knew what to call
Nature beyond that self-fulfilling and – defeating name,

We would have a language so pure it would require
No mind to contain it, no voice to speak it, no body
To breathe it out of its own air into its own air.

Language clearly either exists or does not exist
Without us. The way you think about it
Is a matter of pure faith, maybe, but the answer you choose

Determines everything. Listen: the moonlight coming down
From the small high office window suddenly changes.
The man, whose eyes are closed, does not notice.

He is kissing the woman's neck and shoulder gently
As he feels at her waist for skirt buttons. But the woman's
Eyes are open. She sees the light grown neither

More nor less but other in the room.
What does she think? The answer is complicated.
The man's tongue on her skin is a current of thought

That flows from her neck to her belly,
And his hands at her waistband are clumsy. She moves to help him
Reach higher on her throat and further around her back

To points where nerves and buttons connect
At that moment of the shifting of the light.
Maybe she does not think anything. Maybe she thinks

His body is changing what her body thinks it sees.
She does not understand what is happening in the air
Between her retinas and the moon. Something out there

Has changed profoundly, but she cannot know that.
She touches the man's shirt buttons, opens his shirt,
Lays her palm on his chest. He shivers. Touching

His nipples, she touches the pit of his belly.
All things in the body are connected, all things in the air,
All things in our breath, but only as long as we breathe.

That's what the voice believes. But the voice is a voice.
It has a vested interest. So does the air, insofar as the light
It transmits is sunlight become moonlight become cloudlight

Filtered through the office window and through
The lenses and corneas and sensitive retinas
And unbelievably complex optic nerves and brain

Of what we call a woman and back again
Through her neck and arms and hands
Into the chest of what we call a man

And down to the inward centre of his belly
We call by no accident *solar plexus*, which bring us
Full circle to the sun again, a trick

Of language justified only by the fact
That the man's hands finally solve the problem
Of the skirt's complexity of buttons, hooks, and zipper.

If you believe there are words without bodies, can you also believe
There are bodies without words? Nevertheless, whatever you believe,
The facts remain facts, as far as his hands can tell,

And they tell what they tell without saying that underneath
The wool skirt and beyond the elastic barrier
Of nylon satin, there lies sensitive flesh

Bicameral as the brain, as left- and right-lobed, equally
Mysterious, natural, named and unnameable, traditionally
Lunar, touched through his hands by his belly's solar light.

XVI

Summers, the boy's family would take him south,
Through hardwoods, then pines, riverland, swampland,
Along mussel-shell roads serpentined by the Tangipihoa

Where his father said his mother's cousins night-poached alligators,
Wading waist-deep in moonlight with a flashlight and a knife.
He sat in the back seat watching the roadside, half visionary

And half bored, like anybody travelling, imagining
His friends at home, imagining his mother
When she was a girl, breaking the algae'd surface

Of that river with her quick white body, diving. He'd seen
Old photographs of this same riverbank, of her
At fourteen in a swimsuit, rising from a homemade diving board,

A plank nailed to a rotted cypress stump,
The water she hung above in the black-and-white picture lead-silver,
Covered with grey lily pads and colourless scum.

Those pictures were an aperture into a half world he half understood:
The girl getting ready to dive was exactly his age,
And it was hard to think of her as his mother, hard

To know if he thought she was pretty or not. Her hair
Was long and hung wet: she'd been in already, down
Into whatever right-angled place the river's surface scum concealed,

And he was still in the back seat, half carsick
And half in love. Grown up and remembering, he'd say
Such moments he was lost in time, thrown into a past

He never even lived: but that would be a lie.
He was not lost in his mother's or any past,
He was lost in the future. Live oaks, moss,

River stink on summer Louisiana wind:
All around him the present was falling apart
In the face of what in this boy was about to be

The human apocalypse of lust – but is not that quite yet,
So he does not call it that. He only thinks
Of the place by the river where that girl his mother

Lifted, wondering where she stood
As the mind of the camera catches her
Parting her legs in midair, her bad dive

Held timeless before the water
Can smack its lead-grey belly against her belly
If she's clumsy enough, or take her deep

Into the scum of itself, where everything that moves
Is feelered and goes where it goes
By pure flesh-hunger remembered against the current.

XVII

Comme ça: they touch, and the snow begins.
In the street, the convertible's window rises, closing its crack.
First you can hear the radio music, then you can't:

Blue moon of Kentucky, keep –
And if you're on the sidewalk and the car hisses past
At the instant of the window's closing, and if

You happen to know the song – *too many ifs* –
It will finish itself in your mind: *keep on shining,*
Shine on the one who's gone and left me blue....

The mind completes what it knows, the old clichéd
Rhyme of the history of unhappy love, lifted over
A fiddle and a mandolin by a voice

Like a dog caught in a barbed-wire fence, the High Lonesome Sound:
Blue moon of Kentucky, keep on shining,
Shine on the one who's gone and proved untrue.

The trick of the song is memory. The trick is to keep
The mind just far enough, but not too far,
From cliché, the fossil history of the heart;

110

From happy love, which has no history; from romance,
Which comes into existence only
Where love is fatal, frowned on

And doomed by life itself.
In the office, the man and woman touch.
Is it enough to say they touch? Will the circle

Of this memory intersect other circles
So that something independent reveals itself?
The man and woman reveal each other:

They touch, then they do not touch.
The man takes off his shirt. The woman
Stands up, and her loose skirt slides

Down the satin of her panties. She steps out.
Arclight through the window deepens into snowlight
And the woman stares at the man's goose-fleshed chest.

The foot of air between them seems so far
She thinks if she reached for him now, she would fall
Into one of the clichés of adultery,

Which has as long a history as possession.
This, she thinks, *is an affair.* She's never had one.
She finds a terror in the word

She could hardly have imagined would be there,
Not the fear of being caught, but of being trite.
This is one of those soap operas she hates.

This is a boring story in a magazine
On a rack in a grocery store.
This is a worn-out joke.

She puts her hands over her breasts
In a gesture of sudden shame
And starts to turn away – but the man

Lays his palms on her belly.
The heat she feels is traditional. It compels her
To touch his face, because it is a force so much

Larger and more enduring than she is.
What she has found is sure
Evidence of a connection in being human

Which everybody knows but nobody names
Without irony, or terror of the pure cliché,
Except here, where the woman bends to the man

And uncovers herself again, and puts her hands
On his hands on her belly, and kisses him while the snow
Crystallizes in the arclit air outside

And the convertible makes its circuit of the square
Holding that old rhyme, repeating,
Completing its strict music inside itself.

XVIII

Outside, the sky and its moon wiped vacant and darkly clean
By massed snow clouds, and the street slicked
With a film of something nameless, neither snow nor ice,

And the cars in the parking lot laminated three shades paler,
And the velocity of the rot in the crabapple brought near
The vanishing point by sudden cold – outside, the voice

Remembers its way to the edge of Mt. Vernon, Ohio, to the roadhouse
Where now the band is playing. The fiddler stands
In a cone of cobalt brilliance shot

Down at his face from an ancient spotlight. Sweat
Glitters unnaturally on his forehead and cheeks, touched
With the depth of that blueness, a colour

Not found in the sky or the sea.
And by whatever art it is that a human conveys
A character, a sense of self to the world, he stands

Alone where the circle of his memory intersects
Everything, where the circle stands unbroken
Where it matters, in the strength of its internal law –

Playing, in other words, the fiddle
For the people who are there now, who have come for this.
He plays a tune they all know, but that only he knows

The way he knows it. It is theirs, it is his,
Nobody in the room cares who it belongs to, as long
As it comes to them sweet and hot and they have enough beer.

Outside the cold gets colder. There are no visible stars.
The wind comes down from a circle of its own making.
How can the voice justify the world to the world,

The hard impenetrable backdrop of the inhuman
With the song that the fiddler bows?
Comme ça: Outside the roadhouse, let's say, a white convertible stops.

Its doors open. The music it carried is off.
Inside, in the crowd, a man stands up, one who belongs there.
He has on Levis and Dingo boots, a plaid cowboy shirt

With opalescent snaps and a silver thread in the weave,
A wide leather belt with a gold steer forged on the buckle,
A white Stetson hat. He goes on-stage, takes a microphone,

The move perfectly casual, random, perfectly planned.
When he turns to the crowd and sings, he is precisely
On cue and pitch, and as the first words

Of the song come out of the PA system,
Four underage men stumble in through the fake swinging doors
And hear it again: *Blue moon of Kentucky, keep* –

This is *the illusion of wonder, the illusion of synchronicity,*
The déjà vu illusion: it is as though the song
Has followed them, or come out of them, and they stand

Reverent in the door of the roadhouse, grinning
At this welcome, or in the amazed shame
Of one who is suddenly loved and suddenly knows it.

XIX

I remember the summer, the dense green shade of the yard,
The old brick house my grandmother lived in, crumbled
By roots of long-suffering ivy and Louisiana mildew.

I was the boy half dead of boredom, of entropy of the soul,
Who circled the lawn catching chameleons in the depth of bamboo hedge,
Insufferable. I suffered myself. I was there.

What was happening in my heart? I could have told you
It hurt. I could have told you I was in love
With something, every second, I did not know how to name,

Much less touch. I think I could have said
When egrets lifted into the sky of my grandmother's yard
From the green-scummed water of the Tangipihoa

I hated them for their whiteness, for the light
Lift of their wingspan, for how they wheeled and vanished.
Everything I loved went on without me.

And when girls walked past on the white oyster-shell road,
I hid in the cool bamboo and spied on their bodies'
New vibration and thrust behind T-shirts. Translucence:

That was the word I did not know, but needed.
I could not have told you how it hurt me to hate
The half-seen hunched-at shapes of the naturally hidden,

114

To wake from an unremembered dream in the crotch-slick
Louisiana night, humid in the groin with the knowledge
That something I could not name had almost touched me.

I hated the pain in my body, I hated my body,
I hated loving whatever it was I loved.
This was the end of my natural life,

Of living the way small animals live
In the womb of grass or water.
I hated what I was born from, earth, mother, father.

I hated imagination, which always outstripped my distinctions,
Which lifted the blinding T-shirts of girls, turned them and me
Inside out. That's just growing up, you say.

Oh, it's all perfectly natural.
That's why I was a boy. That's why it was Louisiana.
That's why egrets floated paired in the sexual air.

That's why, when I found, at the back
Of my grandmother's closet,
A paperback copy of a book

With the front ripped off and read
Of the man's throbbing velvet shaft
And the woman's honeyed hole

And the sweetness of the flowing
Juices, and the good hurt
Of bodies about to be touched,

I knew I loved
One nature and not another,
Knew those words were not

What I was, but what I was fated
To become, countervoice, the ancient argument:
That the body is a way of knowing.

That nerves and skin are one authority
No one sane and living
Will argue with seriously

When it comes right down to the question
Of pain's reality.
That when you kick the stone

The voice you assume
Comes out of your gut so sudden
You forget you believe you subsume

Body in your personal Oversoul.
Let that formal feeling come.
Let the man and woman feel

Imperiously drawn
To the same voice, to the real
Negation of what they think they own

And will not in this life give up owning.
Let them come anyway, not knowing they come
Blind to each other, built to know by touching

And knowing by touching's pain
That nothing is only nothing,
That the voice owns everything.

xx

Now, in the parking lot, miraculously, snow
Precipitates from the air, turns the pair of cars
Left there into beautiful abstractions.

The night inflates with the luminosity of snowfall,
Dim but tangible. The edges of the ugly
Office building harden against what is not sky

But eddies and lacy jags of snowfall suspended
Between you and the actual sky, an illusion of sky
Appearing and falling out of some indeterminate middle distance

No sense of perspective can define. But notice: you
Are here now. The voice has brought you
Obliquely, sucked you in and surrounded you

With a world disappearing as you watch it
Into soft, stark undifferentiation.
This is an act of will. This is a leap of faith.

This is a godlike power that lets you penetrate
Space, mind, time, the brick walls of an office building
You never wondered about before, wherein

The man and the woman face each other.
You move, the walls dissolve, you see her stand
Naked, finally, before him.

The voice holds them for you motionless in a light
Bizarre as X-ray illumination, or an infrared
That lets you see the metaphysically disguised,

But is, after all, only the refracted whiteness
Of snowfall come down through a small high office window.
Yet for now, the scene seems timeless, like a drawing on a wall

Of a cave deep beneath the surface of France, touched suddenly
By the flashlight glow and carbon-14-sensitive instruments
Of archaeologists come to witness and record

And try to understand that when masculine figures appear here
They are always clothed in some sort of costume,
But female figurines are absolutely naked,

Simply standing, unadorned. This, they conjecture,
Says something about the psychological and consequently mythical
Values of the male and female presences: the woman

Immediately mythic in herself
And experienced as such,
Not only as source and giver of life,

But also in the magic of her touch and presence –
Whereas the male, costumed, is one
Who has *gained* his powers

And represents some specific, limited
Social role or function. The man, in fact, is costumed.
He has his pants and shoes on –

Levi's, deck shoes from L. L. Bean – chosen carefully to fit
His sense of years of living to gain and own
Himself, this particular man come to be

Husband somehow, father somehow, respectable businessman,
A good man somehow, a nice man somehow, somehow responsible and kind,
And now somehow about to be the lover

Of this woman who stands before him naked.
And in this connection, suddenly the clothes he still wears seem
Absurd, inappropriate, an insult

To the presences he senses around him – the woman,
The archaeologists with their flashlights,
The voice, and especially *you*,

The illusion who has come here expecting something – so he stands,
Kicks off the shoes easily, bends to slip off the socks,
Struggles for a moment with belt buckle and Levi's button and zipper,

Wrestles the jeans off, slips out of the jockey shorts,
Straightens, and faces the woman.
He is taller than she is, a little. Millions of years

Of natural selection have seen to that. Millions of generations
Have brought them here in their different bodies
And in their nakedness they assume the dignity

Of biological tradition, whose marks are everywhere
On the flesh which possesses them: shape of the penis erect,
Receiving shape of the vagina, shape of the hands

Made to grip, stroke, penetrate: shape of the nerves
Of the skin made ubiquitous, sensitive, inflammable.
Here everything the body is stands effective and revealed

And if she does not think *But I hardly know him*
It is because she is in this relation to him,
Having dropped and scattered everything

Concealing, everything temporal, everything temporary
As home, husband, children – revealing herself
Continuous with the powers we name *light, life, passion* –

In which continuum she knows him perfectly. And he
Does not think anything, having thrown away
The emblems of what he thinks of as himself:

He touches her with the absolute authority
The body, revealed, reveals. History, mythology,
Biology, the art of the family

Suspend as the man and woman move together.
And that might be all, that might be the end of the story,
If the voice chose to let you forget

These truths: that this is the workplace, that you are here
To witness everything, beginning to end,
And since you have given yourself up

To this, *the passionate illusion*, you can only go into the body
Of the act, into the reality of consequence,
Into the life of that slice of the natural world

We choose to call *Mt. Vernon, Ohio,*
Within which and outside of which
Everything that happens here happens.

So now, the man and woman touch and come together
And the egg in her body is ready for the sperm in his,
And maybe their natural children are sleeping in different rooms

Across town from each other, dreaming of a place
Where snow falls and dissolves in the black silence of a stream
That follows itself under winter-dead trees coldly toward the sea.

Walt Whitman in Hell (1992)

...on the black waters of Lethe?
                                    – Ginsberg

In the second circle – the level of perpetual dysfunction
Where untouchable lovers are damned by definition
To read each others' stories over and over

In voices like monotonous tape loops repeating forever
The lessons of the *Book of the Unabridged Living Body* –
The interior lights of a downtown express strobe

Grand Central platform and vanish leaving nothing
But a retinal afterglow of the Lexington Avenue line.
Engines push tarry winds out of the heavy darkness

Of the tunnels. They break like punished hurricanes
Into the station's wintery light. I carry a map
Of this place in memory only – uptown, downtown,

Crosstown – capillaried in the visual mind,
Terminal names a systole and diastole of space
That contracts and relaxes around me when I think of it,

Including everything, the whole corporeal ghost
Of Manhattan and beyond. But where is anything, really?
Do I dare trust memory's directions? Or is this the first

And most damning despair, that it may all be nothing
But dots, biochemical flashes, swampgas waverings
Of imaginary light, the meaning of this landscape

Of ashes simply being that I have to wonder
What it means, and thereby recall myself?
And as if this uncertainty were one of the most sublime

Angels of torture, I am suddenly empowered
To remember the mountains, hills, and gorges
Of Manhattan, where the gates of the subways appear

To the sight like holes and clefts in the rocks,
Some extended and wide, some straitened
And narrow, many of them rugged – they all,

When looked into, appear dark and dusky;
But the spirits in them are in such a luminosity
As arises from burning coals. Someone

Among them plays a saxophone – no, someone scats
A bebop riff in a voice so skewed by sterno
It comes through sounding like brass,

And modulates into the Lydian mode:
Someone of them remembers *A Love Supreme,*
And this is my signal, I go down, and everything begins.

It is given now that I realize what comes first,
The station of instruction, the 81st St. entrance
On the Avenue of the Americas line. I enter

From the basement of the Museum of Natural History,
Where passing over is a simple fact, no astonishment,
Because overhead is a whole granite houseful

Of *memento mori* – tombstones, mummies,
And the ichthyosaur's whatmeworry grin. The way here
Is wide and smooth, passing over is a token

I buy from a woman in a Plexiglas cube,
Passing over is a slot and the click of a turnstile. It is here
The man with the methyl voice sings Coltrane and passes out

Pamphlets enumerating the seven words that mean
The body thinking: Thumos, Phrenes, Nöos, and *Psyche,*
All of them translated variously from Homeric Greek

As *mind* or *soul* – and *Kradie, Ker,* and *Etor,*
Rendered often as *heart* or *spirit.* But all
The translations are wrong, I read, entirely:

These must be thought of as objective parts
Of the body, the pamphlet tells me, understood
As my first clue that I am leaving

Anything behind. I embody now the plains and valleys
Of Brooklyn near the foot of the Brooklyn Bridge,
Where the subway gates resemble dens and caverns,

Chasms and whirlpools, bogs, standing water –
And when they are opened, there bursts from them
Something like the fire and smoke that is seen in the air

From burning buildings, or like a flame without smoke,
Or like soot such as comes from an explosive chimney,
Or like a mist and thick cloud: it is here the woman

With a face like a drowned suicide's crouches
At the first turning of the downward stairway
I can't help choosing, holding up her autocratic

Homemade sign: I AM A VICTIM
OF THE CONSPIRACIES OF NAZI RACIST
HATRED THEY HAVE SEALED MY VAGINA

WITH MOLTEN LEAD AND LEFT ME TO DIE
ALONE THEY SEND MY CHILDREN BACK TO ME
DAILY IN MANILA LEGAL ENVELOPES

PIECE BY MYSTERIOUS PIECE DON'T BELIEVE
A WORD THEY TELL YOU PITY ME.
It is here I feel the first angina-constriction

Deep in the cardiac mind, and the *Nöos* says to the *Psyche,*
Watch where you go once you have entered here,
Which way and to whom you return,

To which the *Kradie* answers, *That is not our concern.*
It is our fate to open every door. So I remember, now,
This is the real truth of it: I enter from every gate

At once, on every numbered street and avenue,
Jackson Heights, Mt. Eden, Bleeker, Lorimer, 59th –
And the enormity of my multitudinousness,

This apocalyptic rush hour, eclipses even the brilliance
Of the four quarters of the midnight city –
Regions with designations, attributes, and enumerations:

North the Quarter of the Vomiting Multitudes,
East the Quarter of Suppurations, *West*
The Quarter of the Pissing Millions, *South* the Quarter

Of Investment Banking – but before I can say them,
The great fluid weight of my entering
Washes me forward, and the silent electric doors

Of the silver cars open all together to take me in,
Every human soul of me at every intersection
In every borough of the city, bringing me in a thunderous

Convergence of superimposed switch-engines
Simultaneously *here*, to a level that demands me,
Grand Central Terminal, and the carriers disgorge me

In my statistical millions to circle
From platform to platform where the right trains
Never come. Every man and woman who was breathing

An instant ago must be with me now. Here is the tourist
From Michigan – she was staring at the Empire State
When a cloud of noxious oblivion touched her,

And she opened her eyes and was part of me.
Here is the lawyer from Queens; he knew the city
Inside out, but now he wanders this station

He passed through hundreds of times in his life
Wide-eyed and blank, dangling his forgotten briefcase
Like the ghost of a severed limb. Here is the man

Who bewildered, here is the child who devoured,
Here is the old Hindu woman who lived
Sweetly as a saint, and woke to this at ninety

From a heart-bursting sexual dream, the perfect
Circle of the caste mark between here eyes
Red as a cartoon bullet hole.

Here is the stockbroker, here is the stewardess,
Here is the crowd of girls with prep school sweaters
And haloes of frosted hair who seem to be joined at the waist.

Here is the Chinese couple who juggled feathers
At the Lincoln Centre Circus – they move
Their disciplined hands together, seeking a familiar balance.

Here is the Chilean ex-diplomat who went in fear
Of CIA assassins – to him these tiled walls
Have a beautiful coolness, he's never been so calm.

Here is the defrocked priest: forgetfulness
Has utterly altered him. Here is the ex-Reagan aide:
She seems completely unchanged.

And the Priestess of Greenwich Village,
And the slacker, and the dental assistant,
The majorette, the machinist, the freak, and the mother's son –

This is more than consent, or concord; it is a real
Unity of us all, in one and the same person,
Made by covenant of all of us with each of us, in such a manner

As if each of us should say to all of us, *I Authorize.*
I am a random human diorama, an out-take
From *The Night of the Living Dead.* This is my punishment

For forgetting to believe that blankness is the logical
Outcome of my passionate confusions. Now chaos darkens
The holy brightnesses of the unconscious world.

Overhead, signs light up to enumerate directions and destinations:
A Lake of Fire. A Bottomless Pit. A Horrible Tempest.
Everlasting Burnings. A Furnace of Fire. A Devouring Fire.

A Prison. A Place of Torments. A Place of Everlasting
Punishment. A Place where People Pray. A Place
Where they Scream for Mercy. A Place where they Wail.

A Place where they Curse God. In the vastnesses
Of Sotheby's, snuffboxes, folk arts, antiquities, toys,
Judaica, and other sacred artifacts take on

An unearthly luminosity – at the Village Gate,
The horns of fusion musicians synthesize and burn.
Now the imperious *Phrenes* begins to thrash

Far down in the shadows of the diaphragm,
The intercostal muscles of the rib cage, the smooth
Muscles surrounding the bronchial tubes

That regulate their bore, and so their resistance
To the passage of air – and beside it, or within it,
Its Siamese-twin *doppelgänger* image or other self,

The terrible *Thumos,* also snorts out of a primitive dream
Of breath-souls and the smooth interiors
Of ventricles and veins, black bile and yellow bile, mucous

And vitreous humours. They surface together
Like incestuous homoerotic lovers waking hours
Before sunrise, both blind and invisible,

Caught in a bedroom-darkness so profound
They might be sealed in the flesh-insulated cavity
Of one enormous torso. They begin their old dialogue,

The equivalent of the talk of husbands' and wives'
Did you hear a noise? Did you take out the garbage?
Did you pay the gas bill? Are the children murdered? –

But spoken in something other than words,
Whatever the language of nerves and corpuscles
Consists of, which cannot be rendered in the syntax

Of consciousness, but whose faintest echo
Translates roughly [*Phrenes*] *If the body vanishes,*
How can the spirit be broken? [Thumos] Don't ask.

Its scars leave residues. [Phrenes] But if it is the body
That breaks, how long does it take for the heartbeat
To calcify? [Thumos] Hush. Tell me the story

Of the place breath goes to survive
The suffocations we make for it. [Phrenes] It is a place
Where they can never repent, a place of weeping,

A place of sorrows, a place of outer darkness,
A place where they have no rest, a place of blackness
Or darkness forever, a place where their worm dieth not,

And fire is not quenched. [Thumos] And none of this is certain?
But nobody answers, for now the darkness modulates,
And I find I am in a space exterior to the body after all,

On a secret path along the rim of the starless city, perhaps,
Between the wall and the torments, or perhaps in a tunnel
Dug far below the other shafts, where I have been

Let down through a column that seems of brass,
Descended safely among the unhappy that I might witness
The vastation of souls. A multitude of pitiful

Men and women are gargoyled by homelessness here,
Hung in various ways from the different parts of themselves
Corresponding to the sociology of their births.

And the *Thumos* says to the *Phrenes: Enumerate*
The ways the human body can be warped
By punishments, political or metapolitical, and how

Those punishments make allegories of suffering.
Do so succinctly, in an orderly way, clearly,
And giving examples. And the *Phrenes* offers up

This answer: *These are the measure for measure*
Hanging retributions against the disenfranchised:
Those who are Guilty of Passion

Or Cleanliness shall be hung by the pubic hair;
They shall be hung by the pierced thighs, Those
Who are Guilty of Standing Erect; by the eyes

Those who have Seen Things Clearly; by the nose
Those who Smell the Death of the Rat in the Wall;
Those Convicted of Worthiness shall be hoisted

By the reputation; Those Convicted of Intelligence
By the delicate inner skin of the wallet; by the tongue
Those who know Poverty, Hunger, Colour, or Charm;

By the ears Those who Learn the Direction
Of the Class Dialectic; by the genitals Those
Refused Credit; by the breasts Those Discovered

Suckling More of Their Own Kind; by the DNA,
Those who Combine Unfitness with Survival;
By the Phrenes, the ones who are Poor and Disbelieve;

By the Thumos, the Ones who are Poor and Believe.
From the safety of my vantage point, I see
The truth of it all. The damned are ranged

Before me, row on blighted row. I approach the first
Prisoner or corpse or dead soul, a man dangled
By the tissues of the soft palate for the felony

Of his native tongue – he is effigied in the black rags
Of an ancient uniform of the Ohio National Guard,
His empty eye sockets ringed with kohl and stuffed

With planted Colombian Gold, the parchment
Of his forehead tattooed with the nine mystical numerals
Of the cabala of Social Security

And the Kent State coat of arms. In horror
Of this blasphemous apparition, I fall back,
Nearly fainting, and stagger into a landscape

Where five hundred thousand blasted acres
Have been ripped apart by trenches and shells,
Villages cast down in ruins as if by earthquake,

Wounded trees, limbless and headless, looming
Above the desolation like scaffolds, the valley
A skeleton without flesh, save for the bodies

Of half a million dead ground up beneath the ceaseless
Bombardments. In insensible confusion, I stumble
On the misery of women moaning in parlours, in memory

Of the names of rivers their husbands died for –
The Nile, the Rhone, the Rhine, the Somme, the Marne,
The Aisne, the Yser, the Meuse, the Chickamauga,

The Yangtze, the Mekong, the Tigris and the Euphrates,
Where stealth bombers and F-111s vomit sulphur and acid
On the Mesopotamian plain until the image of my old father

Gilgamesh lurches out of the dust to lay hands on
The Byzantine levers of a T-72 Soviet tank. One
Of these demons of unforgetting, a magnetized girl of twenty

Who lived sixty years beyond the day of her lover's desertion
By fuel-air bomb in the wreckage of Panama City,
Comes forward to comfort me with bandages and morphine,

Cool hands on the brow. The story of her girlhood
Materializes within me, an immaculate marriage
Of nightmare and menses. Now the voices of my stillborn

Sons and daughters rise from the blistered tarmac,
The strangled books of the vanished poets of America –
Lindsay, yes, and Sandburg, my binary idiot clones, but louder

I hear sweet Edwin Rolfe, whom no one now remembers:
John's deathbed is a curious affair, he is singing,
The posts are made of bone, the spring of nerves,

The mattress bleeding flesh. Infinite air,
Compressed from dizzy altitudes, now serves
His skullface for a pillow. In my drugged fever dream,

I am damned to the furious realm of Sol Funaroff, where
The earth smoked and baked; stones in the field
Marked the dead land: coins taxing the earth,

And to Countee Cullen's crucifixion:
"Maybe God thinks such things are right."
"Maybe God never thinks at all...."

It seems the body is scattered over the whole expanse
Of thought, arms and legs sliced away and dropped
Horribly into a pail, the circuitry of the nerves

Corroded, abdominal cavity looted for spare parts
And salvage, the *Kradie* and the *Ker*
At infinite removes from one another,

The *Psyche* bereft of the *Etor* – body and body politic
Forever dissevered, like precincts of the brain
In the wake of a bad lobotomy. I try to remember

Wholeness, the image of meadows in starlight,
Lovers in sentimental landscapes, glacier-capped
Purple-skewed mountains, the visionary wheathead

Held up by the Dionysian priest at Eleusis,
The imperious cliché of the sea, the splendid material love
Of Rukeyser – *I have gained mastery*

Over my heart / I have gained mastery
Over my two hands / I have gained mastery
Over the waters / I have gained mastery

Over the river – but it splinters in a billion diffractions,
Cells, dustmotes, atoms of asthmatic pollen,
Spume, sperm, fragments of quartzite, nitrogen,

Duct tape, cotter pins, subatomic wreckage,
Shreds of pointless false narratives left over
From childhood memories or from moon-illumined

Bedrooms where lovers defected from one another's countries.
This is the critical whirlwind. Nothing holds here.
I fracture again and again, giving in to every mythology.

The shattered ghosts come thick. Submicroscopic,
I seep through cracks in the nuclei,
An insidious multitudinous radioactive dust,

Undetectable by any instrument except as an oscillation
The cosmos emits at its own dismemberment
Into particles, into bodies carrying bowls of goats' blood,

Each going down into the hell of its own one-track mind.
Here is the ruptured anarchist soul
Of Arturo Giovanetti in prison, the one true confession

Of his poetry: *Wonderful is the supreme wisdom of the jail*
That makes all think the same thought. / Marvellous
Is the providence of the law that equalizes all, even

In mind and sentiment. / Fallen is the last barrier of privilege,
The aristocracy of the intellect. / I, who have never killed,
Think like the murderer; / I, who have never stolen, reason

Like the thief. What is this place where wisdom
Is an unnatural abomination, all knowledge is nature
Destroyed? How have I come to this perigee, where the heart

Is nothing but a spring, and the nerves but so many strings,
And the joints but so many wheels, giving motion
To the whole, as was intended by the artificer?

Here the larynx of Mike gold, dipped in solder
And traced with magnificent circuitry, picks up the broadcast
His own crushed poems repeat into the emptiness

Like a satellite beacon: *I am resigning from the American legion*
It reminds me of a dog I used to have
That picked up toads in her mouth. . . .

Now, as the voices of these my emanations bark and bleed,
It is the intense strangeness of the world I want
To remember how to love – how it enters and exits

The body, air and ether and light – and to which I long
To return. Thrown into being out of the centre of being.
But what am I – an insulated ghost, appearance, apparition,

Epiphenomenon, holographic projection,
A comic book death's-head cast up on the shore
Of the living? Even this skin, which once trembled

At the thought of the touch of another human body,
Is unreal, only the projection of a vanished surface:
And the mind, when it falters and croaks –

I speak with authority now – loses its shape
As a bodily ego, follows the carcass
Cell by carrion cell, down through vegetable ooze

And crust and maggoty mantle and magma,
And arrives, in the innermost circle
Of the Republic of the Disappeared, at emptiness.

It was here, in the Land of the Metaphysically Free,
That, fallen, I dreamed my old America. By an act
Of most imperial will I assumed the Presidency of the Dead,

I shaped the ruptured shrapnel of my consciousness
Once more into a seedy mercenary army –
Phrenes and *Thumos* and *Nöos*

Commanding rank and file of the husks
Of riveters and lawyers (I gathered them
Tenderly as they settled), and residues of secretaries,

Dregs of ushers, gynaecologists, thieves,
And the fine ash of Iraqi cabdrivers,
And the delicate grit of Marines,

Dust of Bush, Baker, Schwarzkopf, Cheney,
And beautiful Colin Powell: such a clay they made,
Such a multitude moulded, such drum-taps and battle hymns.

At last I believed I understood them. At last
When I called their names they seemed
To shiver to hear me, as if they were almost alive.

But when I look now, there is only the finitude
Of nothing, only absence. I stand in the ultimate circle,
The innermost hell of all the hells, beyond

The outermost illusion: Purity, uncorrupted
Conscience, the body politic embracing
Self and nothing other, only the singular desire.

And as if at a mystical chime, or the alarm
Of a mineral clock, the subway signals ring again,
And I rush at the speed of darkness

From station to station, though the gnarly strata,
In among the tunnels of volcanic roots and sealed absolutes
Of salt domes, up along the nether edges

Of the limbo of flushing, transformed at Queensboro Plaza
And again at Hoyt-Schermerhorn, to emerge at last
In mercuric February afternoon light

At the stairway marked *Brooklyn Bridge*.
Nothing has changed. Manhattan grinds on,
Gears of the living irreversibly meshed

With the ratchet of desire. There is still the apocalyptic
Discharge of cluster-bombs over the lower east side,
Brimstone of artillery out of the Village, sniper fire

From the Chrysler Building, the strafing
Of Bloomingdales. But everything on the earth I love
Is sealed from my touch as by a zone

Of Platonic plate glass. In my loneliness I rise
And hover over the plutonium-grey span
Of East River, licked by the harrowing fallout

Of my own intangibility. From here I can see,
Like a skyline, the obvious contour of all
My error. O I freely confess it now: America,

I was wrong. I am only slightly larger than life.
I contain mere conspiracies. What do I know?
There is no identity at the basis of things, no one

Name beneath all names. There is no more than this
To remember: *It is not godlike to die. It is not even human.*
Refuse the honour, no matter who tells you its conquest is sublime.

I may have mumbled that old lie myself once.
I have confessed to many things. Maybe that is why I am
The only one dead here. Maybe that is why I have to suffer

Everything I can. Maybe that is why –
Over the unconscious roofs of your living
Beauty shops, sweatshops, pawnshops, printshops, meat shops,

Warehouses, bathhouses, crackhouses, penthouses, card houses –
Once and for all unhearable, and for all I know unthinkable, I go on
Sounding my doomed eternal bodiless goddamned

Half-Life Studies (1999)

1.

A handful of powder can break a city's back,
    a scatter of sleet, cloudlight, luminescence of salt.
At the taxi stand, a driver from Senegal practices
    thinking in English. *Etoile*, he whispers. *No: star.*

Star, snow, diesel, moon, fatherland, wing,
    and the mystical incantation *carburettor.* Inside, beyond
Plate glass, a man and a woman stick in the throat
    of a life, in the gut of an argument, and one girl in pink

Is possessed by the Demon of the Grecian Urn.
    Atlanta airport: Every snowbound flight shuts down.
Nobody's going anywhere. Bursts of bar conversation
    syncopate into sniper fire: *Nice little culture*

You got here. / If God intended folks to fly, we'd be born
    with more reservations. Dangerous vortices of rage
Burn on Doppler screens. Everyone here wants transcendence.
    No life in the moment. Bodiless lift. The lyric's

Poisonous glow. The father of the girl in pink
    feels the ticket in his jacket pocket discharge
Its singular pulse of frustration. The mother breathes
    on the window and draws a cartoon face which fades

As she watches. Through its left hemisphere she silhouettes
    the taxi driver against his yellow rime-scummed Ford.
He, in turn, remembers the face of his own mother transfixed
    in the doorway the morning he took the road to Dakar

And the rotting shipyard. Then the sick grind of ocean. Then
    The Convention Centre. She is still standing there,
Expressionless, almost swallowed in empty shadow.
    She will never move again. *United*, he thinks, *Las Vegas*, meter

Not running, each snowflake a punctuating loss.
Coca-Cola. Please direct me to Peachtree Street.
Multiple avenues to salvation. De-icer. What's your angel's name?
Whiteness fouls every access road in sight.

2.

She lies in bed in a strange city, watching
   her lover while he sleeps, someone else's
Books on the shelves, strangers' snapshots
   framed on the bureau: a coal train
on its track along a river fixed in black

   acid against limestone – a Toyota
At curbside, fading, releasing its ghostly odour
   of bromide – anatomy of branches
Through a window, smudged against pale sky.
   She is living in an old photograph,

A fin-de-siècle tintype, brown-edged, slightly
   out of focus. When the sunlight
Makes its way across the comforter to touch her,
   she feels herself begin to disappear.
Her palms go first, clarifying like lenses. Then

   her legs – daguerreotype of a wartime amputee.
Chemistry is merciless, her aura helpless
    in this light. When the man wakes,
There is nothing beside him but a face, oddly
   faded, familiar in a distant way —

An ancestor maybe, distorted behind old glass
   in a gold-foil frame – or nobody,
A child in a porch swing who never had a name,
   never had a life, not even forgotten, regarding him
With a crudely fixed gaze, colourless but certain.

3.

When she wakes one morning, *Mood Indigo* is playing
    on the radio at the back of her mind.
Rain blows, too, in distant courtyards, its small music
    sharp against deserted benches and quartz-
veined flagstones. In the steeple across the boulevard
    it touches the chapel bell. Resonance. *Mood Indigo*:
Behind the ballroom door of the medulla oblongata,
    all the dead musicians lift their nerveless horns.
Or is there just a radio after all, sitting on a hallway table—
    a mahogany RCA with an incandescent dial
The lovers forgot when they went downstairs to mix
    another gin and tonic in the kitchen? No matter.
The horns stay lifted. And the syncopation of rain plays on
    against the window of this room where other instruments
Measure the rhythm of her blood, the strange counterpoint
    of cell against cell. Nurses' carts. Interns humming.
So many years that scalpel and ether can't control
    take shape in a nonexistent saxophone's bell.
She could make a theory of it, or at least a religion,
    if she could only move her hands again.
Trombones in a garden. A set of drums in the bedroom.
    Behind a curtain, lovers forgetting to breathe.

4.

He remembers the little train
    in the beautiful country—
Massed green of forests, stone-lined
    fields, then apricot trees,

A wooden pen, a goat. Villages.
    Larkspur. A small
Iron footbridge over the tracks.
    And on a garden bench,

Asleep, intricately folded in
	on herself like a Swiss
Army knife, his mother the eight-
	armed goddess. Today

He sits alone in the curry shop
	trying to read the news.
Blowing rain against plate glass:
	hours, and nobody comes

For pakora, vindaloo, aloo saag.
	An ambulance screams past,
A Volvo, two starving dogs, a bearded
	holy woman with a sign

In illegible French, magic
	marker words half destroyed
By weather. Wiping a palm
	on his white chef's coat,

He thinks of the land scrolling past,
	his father vigilant
At the third-class window.
	Groaning and rattling,

The train made its dark incision
	in the belly of the world.
He was only a boy, dressed in his best
	white suit, sucking cheap candy.

What could he do against the anaesthetic
	green of an alien country?
His life is not a bad life now.
	On his wall one Jesus,

One Shiva, one Buddha. It is
	his life. Nothing in it
Shames him. But he must not forget
	his father's eyes seared

With intelligent sadness.
      And when he thinks
Of his mother, it is necessary to see
      The eyes of a goat—

Gold flecks against darkness, weird
      vertical slit of pupil
Intent on dangerous difference—
      and the anonymous look

On the face of the goddess as she lifts
      the animal's chin to bare
The throat, the impersonal blessèd knife
      borne suddenly down.

5.

Just as the rain begins, a man dressed as a priest
      steps out of a café doorway onto the sidewalk, moving
As if there were no such thing as weather, down the avenue
      where shop windows display all the worldly goods
We are told we must give up. A priest, or a man
      dressed as a priest? Rain, or chemistry dressed as rain?
Hands invisible in his cassock sleeves, he walks without looking
      left or right or even before him, head down
In an attitude of brooding or meditation or constant prayer.
      He passes the boy with no legs singing for coins
In the shadow of a shoeshop's sign, the woman in mink hiding
      her face indignantly from the rain in her priceless collar.
Emblems are everywhere, and he makes his way among them
      respectfully but with determination, as if his lifelong training
Were in techniques of proper relation to surfaces and their meanings.
      Suppose he carries a copy of *The Cloud of Unknowing* wrapped
In bookshop paper hidden in an inner pocket? Suppose
      he carries a copy of *Das Kapital*? The café waiter
Deferred to him, brought him an extra serving
      of excellent bouillabaisse with honest peasant bread.

The soul of a priest is nothing to a waiter, as long
    as the food is free. The waiter's mother was a beauty
In her youth, took many lovers, died embittered and faithless,
    broken by loss of face. No one to blame, no one to forgive.
Memento mori are worth whatever price. Now the waiter clears
    the table, lifting saucer and soup bowl, brushing crumbs away.
No tip. His reward will be beyond the surgeon's shop, the brothel,
    the Temple of Apollo, in the fogbank at the avenue's end.

Axis (2000-2001)

Martin Heidegger's reputation as one of the greatest philosophers of the 20th century rests largely on his first book, *Sein und Zeit* (*Being and Time*), published in Germany in 1927, which takes "the Meaning of Being" as the terrain of its inquiry and Dasein (being-there) as that inquiry's focus. The term *Dasein* takes on special significance for Heidegger's phenomenological study. "*Dasein* is an entity which does not just occur among other entities. Rather it is ontologically distinguished by the fact that, in its very Being, Being is an issue for it" (*Being and Time*, Blackwell 1962, trans. Macquarrie and Robinson, 32). Furthermore, "*Dasein* is not only close to us – even that which is closest; we *are* it, each of us, we ourselves. In spite of this, or rather for just this reason, it is ontologically that which is farthest".

In recent years, abundant evidence has proven that Heidegger was a Nazi — a party member who was for a time put in charge of the restructuring, along party lines, of the German university system (see, for instance, Victor Farias's *Heidegger and Nazism*, [Temple UP, 1991]). In this fact, obviously, lies the nub of an ethical conundrum for anyone interested in Heidegger's philosophical work.

> *Every inquiry is a seeking. Every seeking gets guided beforehand by what is sought.*
> – Martin Heidegger, 1899-1976

In Memoriam CVH, 1921-1994

1.1 – IN WHICH HE IS EXTINGUISHED

Nothing in the blood, nothing in the brain,
Nothing in the tongue contains us at the end.
How was it this man died? Completely.
He breathed into concealment. Or concealed
His way into unbreathing. He was and then
Was not. Even a death can be normal, common.
Even a death can feel familiar. He turned unreal
As I watched him. Right in front of me

He transformed himself into an ordinary shadow.
And that was a death to die for: transparent, compact,
Unbeautiful but unassuming. Almost abstract.
His lyric ended. He was just a dead man now,
Untouched by starlight, storms, wings, scythes, harps.
His last words were *I want to be a corpse.*

1.2 — IN WHICH HE IS CREATED

In the idea of the past, on the threshing floor
Of history just south of the primal hut,
A grandmother throws down her bushel of sorry wheat.
Around her a luminosity of motes — above her
A kind of solitary weather we have forgotten how to name,
Grim in its atmospherics, bearing the bruise of God
From sky to river to face to stone to colourless cloud —
And behind her an evolution so heartless it had to become

The story of what passes for destiny among the chosen.
Unthinking, she scatters her grain; unthinking, she murders
An age of the world. All this for a little flour.
All this for a loaf of chaffy bread. She threshes. And soon
Out of the dust and sweat of her filthy labour
A shape appears, which she slaps into breath: my father.

1.3 — IN WHICH HE DENIES HIMSELF

This child is a disbeliever. The motherland
And fatherland never did those things to each other.
Awful things. Awful bodies. He understands
He came from somewhere. But if love negates the lover,
Why be here? If he ran away from himself,
It would all still be as lovely as it is, the wheatfield
Would go on ripening its floury half-life,
The forest grow darker, its creatures more richly concealed

In the absence he would leave behind.
Poor little childless father. He wants to wipe away
Memories of scenes he never saw. He wants to unremember
The trench he crawled out of, the unmothering machines
That convoyed him down from heaven the day
He invaded this dimension and declared himself a war.

1.4 — IN WHICH HE IS CLARIFIED

To the east of him, therefore, a phalanx of tractors
Advances, camouflaged against the margin of the forest –
To the west, threshers triangulate the torn theatre
In which grain blitzes its fated ripeness
Out of the ground of its own being, and retreats.
Nothing is neutral, not sweat, rot or erosion.
His enemy creates him. A V-formation of geese,
A platoon of cattle: everything is explosion,

No no man's land. And as for his childhood,
His orders are clear: you can have it as long
As you can hold it. Mother and father and God
Are good, but something familiar and wrong
Breaks holy ground in the blood.
He prays to his Father in his mother tongue.

2.1 — IN WHICH HE RECEIVES A DESIGNATION

From the other side of the earth, in the Holy City
Of Thought, the Philosopher of Being regards
My tiny father through the transparent indeterminacy
Of a glittering logical lens inflicted on him by the gods.
Turning it awkwardly and squinting, able to measure
The child's position that way, or else his velocity –
First one, then the other, never the two together –
He begins the outline of a hypothetical biography,

Or hagiography perhaps. Here is a boy
Born in ignorance, stunned by Being, thrown
Out of nowhere into the centre of a horrible story
Being written around him in blood, by no one.
The Philosopher smiles. His inquiry is plain.
At the top of a fresh page, he writes my father's name: *Dasein*

2.2 — IN WHICH HE IS ECLIPSED

On the Continent of the Philosopher,
The Axis is revolving.
Or the Continent resolves around it:
This problem needs either solving
Or ignoring; the Philosopher is unsure.
And he is distracted. Heavy machinery
Grinds in the dark outside the city gate,
And smoke obscures the scenery,

That same mysterious smoke.
Surely it has a source. Perhaps the trains.
Trains are everywhere now, a mechanical vermin,
Like the laundry truck at the corner, like the tank
At the city centre. Much is obscure.
But the obscure fascinates him. That, at least, is clear.

2.3 — IN WHICH HE IS POSSESSED

His jacket is tweed but cheap and worn.
It is cold in the city, and the soldiers are a problem
Of an unphilosophical nature. The Philosopher could have sworn
By the age of thirty he'd have arrived at the apophthegem
That would summarize the cosmos. Matters stand otherwise.
Matters, in fact, are disastrous. Writing comes slow,
Thought slower still. The meaning of the universe
Does not quite *elude*, but exacerbates his mind somehow,

While the Meaning of the University has grown as obvious
As the nose on the face of — well, one of *them*.
Time to get on with it. Time to take care of business.
But this perfect, ignorant boy in his brain — what to do with *him?*
The market is full of soldiers. There are tanks at the edge of town.
Time is getting away from him. He scowls and writes that down.

144

2.4 — IN WHICH HE IS DEFINED

Or: in the deepest, most numinous, most inaccessible space
Of mind, the Philosopher apprehends that very Being
Of which he is the Philosopher: my father's intaglioed face,
Rising up as it does all unexpected and glowing
With intention out of concealment. It implies
Nothing less than everything. So much labour
Of the spirit for something so elemental? Yes.
All over the Continent, the perimeters of the coming war

Appoint themselves. There is evidence: black stacks
At all points of the horizon belch indelible smoke.
What are they burning out there? the Philosopher asks.
But this he does not write down. His work,
He intuits, is Other. The conquest of Otherness.
This genius is a bastard? This bastard is a genius.

3.1 — IN WHICH HE REACHES A LIMIT

Dasein cannot dream the Philosopher. All Being long
He will never think this thought: the dream can dream
The dreamer dreaming. The boy he is belongs
With the animals; the man he will become
Belongs among men. It is simple that way, and clean.
Only in one's mother tongue can one express one's own
Peculiar hatred. His is of the elements, of carbon against carbon.
He is already growing into it. The pure machine

Of conscience will roll over him and he will not recognize it.
What passes in him for innocence requires another definition,
A new hierarchy of spirit. But no one dares devise it.
He is the minister of compost; he is the eggshell king,
Commander of lyric droppings, master of decomposition.
Like a good boy he does his chores, unconsciously uncomplaining.

3.2 — IN WHICH HE IS CONCEIVED

Father is a form. Forgetting this,
We utter him at our peril.
Likewise *sun*, a brilliant, imperious
Form, almost — but only almost — indestructible:
For *God* too is a form, and *peril*, and *forgetting*,
Water and *war*, *animal* and *Dasein*.
Likewise everything you can think of: penetrating
Form, like a bullet in the brain.

Utter him, then, and risk your life: a war
Becomes my father. He is still a tiny form,
Insignificant. He is crossing the great water
In utero at the age of twenty, waiting to be born
Heroic, monstrous in his mother's blood, to save
The world. Or at least to be born alive.

3.3 — IN WHICH HE IS ILLUMINATED

In the middle of an ordinary midnight, in the middle of an ocean,
Dasein leans on a ship's rail and lights a Lucky Strike.
Match-bronzed, he is simply himself, a self-authenticating phenomenon
Etched in scrubbed brass and khaki, backlit, moonstreaked,
Handsome as a film strip, a military classic.
He thinks precisely nothing. There is nothing to be thought.
That is the beauty of it. What is, is. The ship's wake
Glows cinematically, a sentimental symbol shot

In black and white and set beneath a headline.
He has come out of concealment and is lingering here.
He has a purpose. He is full of intention,
And his body is bright with it. You can see it in the way the moon
Arcs the filmy emptiness above him. He is the luminous centre
Of the world beyond the birth canal. Speak, friend, and enter.

3.4 — IN WHICH HE BECOMES THE WORD

My father's language steams across the ocean,
A mechanical fogbank of suspect rhymes: *human,*
Hydrogen, broken, noun, bone, machine.
It is returning to its homeland to investigate its own
Caesarian beginnings. Knife in the belly. Bloody origin.
It wants to kill. It wants all compromising information
Dead. Otherwise, what *is* a mother tongue, a nation?
Its syntax beats in the heart of the ship, a passion

For form that would murder its own son,
Then invent the word *sacred* to explain what it had done.
But my father on the deck requires no explanation.
Holy war, cleansing war, genocide or revolution,
It is his. His mind is his language, but a war
Is circumstance; it demands its metaphor.

4.1 — IN WHICH HE IS BETRAYED

The Philosopher sits at his desk in his underwear.
Rain on his study window deposits a residue
He's never noticed before. He observes in wonder.
What is the Being of rain? Once he thought he knew,
But something in it now reminds him curiously
Of that little colleague — what was he, a theologian,
A Cabbalist? – who came with his hat in his hand, desperately
Asking a favour. Impossible to grant it. And then

The man vanished as if he had never been.
He and his whole family. Rumour had it they'd taken a train
Somewhere into the heartland. Never heard from again.
Pleasant little fellow. Rumour had it he played the violin.
Turned into smoke right there on the threshold: vaporized.
Nothing left but his hat, which is just the Philosopher's size.

4.2 — IN WHICH HE IS OBSCURED

The Philosopher scorns such phenomena. The Axis
Is his concern. What sits at the Centre of Being
Governing Being's revolution? Whatever it is,
He will name it. It is there, just beyond his perceiving.
The Axis is time. The Axis is not time. The Axis is the margin
Along which the war between humanity and God is fought.
Being turns on the Axis; the soul is the heat of its friction.
Or: the Axis impales the world, and the world spins, caught

On a core of pure, dispassionate pain. But another thought
Disturbs him: has the Axis vanished — eroded,
Absconded, collapsed? Or perhaps it *never was*? Still,
Something turns us. And language alone is not
The Axis. It may have another name, but it is *there*: corroded
By God's neglect or human error, but provable, real.

4.3 — IN WHICH HE IS COMPLETED

Now the great ship brings *Dasein* ashore.
He walks the plank and sets foot on the Continent.
He is ready. This is his personal war.
He is being born for it. Nothing can prevent it.
Does the air resist his approach? Does the Continent tremble?
Who can tell? When *Dasein* takes one step,
An artillery shell dissolves a cathedral.
Another step, and a tank platoon blows up

An orphanage. Thus, inch by inch, his advance.
Thousands vanish, revolved into concealment.
Dasein waves them on. Their Axis is a circumstance
He can do nothing to help them circumvent.
Dying's not so bad, the joke goes, *just don't be
Around when it happens*. Bombs fulfil that prophecy.

4.4 — IN WHICH ALL IS EXPLAINED

And everything will remain — that's the mystery:
Whole cities untouched, whole continents undisplaced.
Beyond the ordnance and the massive machinery,
Everything that is happening is merely commonplace.
The armature of the pelvis funnels one human into Being,
And another, and another. That much, the Philosopher understands.
For the rest of it, who cares what God is doing?
In that question, philosophy ends, and begins.

Stones forget about blood. Blood washes away.
The wind is less than nothing, a nerveless gas. And dust —
What is dust? Trash that makes you sneeze. A cheap cliché.
Why worry that the rain is full of it now? All of this
Is error. The Greeks would agree: the real remains
Real. The rest is explosion, artillery, the rattle of trains.

5.1 — IN WHICH HE IS ABANDONED

The Philosopher dresses himself. He has someplace to be,
An appointment, a rendezvous. His whitest shirt
Calms him. He admires it. And his very expensive tie
Was a gift from someone important. But what about this hat?
He holds it, undecided. It reminds him of something unpleasant,
A half-remembered dream. He looks around him, about to leave,
But something holds him. The flat is perfectly neat,
All the appliances silenced. It's foolish, but he's ready to grieve

For the books arrayed in their perfect jackets, the papers in piles
On the desk, even the clean drapes. How strange, how irrational!
He wants to tell the piano he'll only be gone for a little while —
To another city, yes, a distant country, really nowhere at all....
On the sidewalk, the rain lets down its bony grit.
It's good that he has his hat to protect him from this shit.

5.2 — in which he reads Being and Time

Dasein arrives, expected, at a certain city, in a certain street.
He makes his way through the impure sunrise to a certain door.
It opens at his approach. He enters, confident
That this is the moment he spent so long being born for.
The hatrack is empty, of course. He searches the unpeopled rooms
Following that great sound he hears — foyer, parlour, kitchen,
It grows louder, an immortal golden hum
Like the sound of a galaxy of bees, or an immaculate machine

Stamping the face of God out of immortal alloy.
He finds it in the study, under the books, piercing the floor, the desk,
The ceiling: an antimatter shaft or negative axle, cusp
Around which the flat, the world, is spun: climax of the story,
Axis at last, grinding, numinous, omnipotent.
Dasein studies it, frowning, then finds the off-switch and flips it.

5.3 – in which he vanishes

Time to die. Something in his brain
Dictates it. Some grubby little *führer*
In the genes gives the order
And the synapses fire. Bedpan,
Morphine, scalpel, hearse in the rain:
Details merely. I see my father
Turn to ash, or turn the corner
At the end of the last street in the city of *Dasein*.

He turns his back. Away. He prepares
The corpse within him, and then becomes it: *turns
Into it*, as we say. Our words turn on us. Crematoria burn
Discreetly in our cities. He would have it so: no stars
Obscured by his rising, no carbonized trace
In the weather of his stillborn, unimportant face.

5.4 — IN WHICH HE BECOMES AN APOLOGIA

So the end of history comes, and nothing happens.
The landscape goes on, oaks beside trenches beside sheep;
Morning shows up in the cities; the markets open;
Children stumble to school, shell-shocked by the usual sleep.
Railroads keep their schedules; conductors erase
Certain recent destinations and begin speaking kindly
To the passengers again. Churches forgive even the priests –
It is worth any price to have an ordinary Sunday

With the ordinary sins committed and confessed.
We converse with each other again, just as we had done –
Well, always really. Has anything intervened?
There are fewer of us now, but surely there always have been.
Here and there a crater — hospital, house, mysterious ruin –
But we have jobs and gods again; we are serious, and blessed.

T. R. Hummer was born in Macon, Mississippi in 1950 and grew up in rural Noxubee County on a farm. He attended the universities of Southern Mississippi and Utah before embarking, in 1980, upon a career of teaching literature and creative writing at a number of academic institutions including the University of Oregon, where he was director of the creative writing programme.

Hummer has published eight full-length collections of poetry, and is also known as a short story writer, essayist and reviewer, his work appearing in such publications as *The New Yorker* and *Harper's* and in leading literary journals.

The recipient of a Guggenheim Fellowship and a National Endowment for the Arts Fellowship, he has twice won the prestigious Pushcart Prize for his poetry.

In 2001, Terry Hummer became the editor-in-chief of the University of Georgia's prize-winning literary journal, *The Georgia Review*.

Also available in the
ARC PUBLICATIONS
International Poets series

LOUIS ARMAND (Australia)
Inexorable Weather

DON COLES (Canada)
Someone has Stayed in Stockholm

SARAH DAY (Australia)
New & Selected Poems

GAIL DENDY (South Africa)
Painting the Bamboo Tree

ROBERT GRAY (Australia)
Lineations

MICHAEL S. HARPER (USA)
Selected Poems

ALAMGIR HASHMI (Pakistan)
The Ramazan Libation

DENNIS HASKELL (Australia)
Samuel Johnson in Marrickville

DINAH HAWKEN (New Zealand)
Small Stories of Devotion

BRIAN HENRY (USA)
Astronaut
Graft

RICHARD HOWARD (USA)
Trappings

ANDREW JOHNSTON (New Zealand)
The Open Window

JOHN KINSELLA (Australia)
Lightning Tree
The Silo:
A PASTORAL SYMPHONY
The Undertow:
NEW & SELECTED POEMS
Landbridge:
ANTHOLOGY OF CONTEMPORARY AUSTRALIAN POETRY
ED. JOHN KINSELLA

THOMAS LUX (USA)
The Street of Clocks

J.D.McCLATCHY (USA)
Division of Spoils

MARY JO SALTER (USA)
A Kiss in Space

ANDREW SANT (Australia)
The Unmapped Page

ELIZABETH SMITHER (New Zealand)
A Question of Gravity

C. K. STEAD (New Zealand)
Straw into Gold
SELECTED POEMS
The Right Thing
Dog

ANDREW TAYLOR (Australia)
The Stone Threshold

JOHN TRANTER (Australia)
The Floor of Heaven